IRAN'S RELATIONS WITH PAKISTAN:

A STRATEGIC ANALYSIS

IRAN'S RELATIONS WITH PAKISTAN:

A STRATEGIC ANALYSIS

Dr. Satyanarayan Pattanayak

(Established 1870)

United Service Institution of India
New Delhi

Vij Books India Pvt Ltd
New Delhi (India)

Published by

Vij Books India Pvt Ltd

2/19, Ansari Road, Darya Ganj
New Delhi - 110002
Phones: 91-11-43596460, 91-11- 65449971
Fax: 91-11-47340674
web : www.vijbooks.com
e-mail   : vijbooks@rediffmail.com

ISBN: 978-93-80177-65-6

CONTENTS

CONTENTS

Foreword

The book, *Iran's Relations with Pakistan: A Strategic Analysis*; by Dr. Satyanarayan Pattanayak, is a timely study of a theme of significant importance in the context of rapidly changing geo-strategic environment in India's immediate neighbourhood. It also throws light upon diplomatic tenacity of two nations on how to pursue long term strategic objectives despite rapidly changing regional and international environment as well as revolutionary changes in domestic politics. The study will be of great help to Indian decision- makers in forming India's West Asia policy.

Since independence, India and Pakistan have been competing for support from countries of West Asia. While Pakistan had harped on common religious ties as also alleged common cultural heritage, India had sought to win over friends on political planks like support during the nationalist movement and anti-colonial struggle, concepts of Arab nationalism and non-alignment. Stress on non-alignment led to an alienation of pro-Western states like Iran and Turkey (as also Iraq before 1958) because of their membership of the Baghdad Pact/ CENTO. India's focus on supporting nationalism and anti-colonialism as also Arab nationalism began to lose its appeal after the decline of Nasserism, more so after the Arab defeat in the Arab-Israeli War of 1967. India had also alienated some Arab states like Saudi Arabia that saw Nasserism as a strategic threat, as also Baathist leaders of Syria and Iraq who viewed Nasserism as a competing ideology. The formation of OIC following the Rabat Conference in 1969 provided Pakistan with a wider political forum thereby further undermining India's political role in the region.

Pakistan's diplomacy in West Asia, of which Pakistan-Iran relations is a part, focuses primarily upon the single-minded Pakistani objective of undermining India's position while gaining political, economic and strategic benefits for itself. Pakistan held on to that objective and even used the changing regional and global environment to pursue its path. In the fifties and sixties it used its links in the Baghdad Pact/CENTO to benefit even strategically during the Indo-Pak military confrontations of 1965 and 1971. It sought to buttress its alignment with these northern tier countries by helping to create the RCD; renamed ECO in 1985. ECO was further expanded in 1992 to include ex-Soviet Central Asia States. During the entire period, Pakistan was able to maintain cordial relations with states like Saudi Arabia and Iran despite the fact that their relations had acquired an adversary proportion after 1979. It was an excellent example of Pakistan's diplomacy of successfully walking on a tight rope even in overtly adverse circumstances.

While analyzing Pak-Iran relations, it is important to place Iran in its historical perspective. Iranian psyche is deeply ingrained with its long civilizational background which makes Iranians proud of their heritage despite the outer-layer of present day Shii radicalism. Iranian influences in the past had enveloped parts of Central Asia, Afghanistan as also parts of what constitutes Pakistan. That gives Pak-Iran relations a special flavor. It has enabled both the countries not only to coexist but also to evolve common approaches to regional problems despite changes in regimes as well as regional and global environment.

Pakistan's diplomacy would not have succeeded if it was not matched and reciprocated by that of Iran. For Iran, the period of the Shah as also of the present regime, Pakistan represented an immediate neighbour on its eastern flank. Iranian regimes had suffered from the threat perception of encirclement by hostile elements. During the days of the Shah, the threat was seen from the USSR in the north, Arabs in the east, and possible threat to Iranian maritime trade and oil lane in the Straits of Hormuz and Gulf of Oman. A stable and friendly Pakistan was, thus, of great strategic significance for Iran, especially when Soviet influence was seen to influence Afghanistan and India.

Iranian ruling elite continued to fear from encirclement even after the Islamic revolution. The Arab threat was soon aggravated by Shia – Sunni divide. Iraq- Iran War and the support of the GCC states to Iraq was seen in that context. Iran's threat perception vis-à-vis USA also increased because of growing US presence in the Indian Ocean and in the GCC States. Soviet presence in Afghanistan also added to that threat of encirclement. Iranians thus, sought friendship of Pakistan, despite the fact that Pakistan had joined the axis of Saudi Arabia and USA to confront Soviet presence in Afghanistan. It must go to the credit of both Pakistan and Iran that they were able to reassure each other despite the fast changing regional environment. Iranians did not make a public issue of Pakistan's close links with USA and Saudi Arabia who were seen as antagonistic to Iranian strategic interests.

Pakistan and Iran were also able to come closer despite the upheavals in Afghanistan, targeting of Shia by Sunni Taliban, and the presence of Al-Qaida that was openly hostile to the Shiism. Pakistan also succeeded in reassuring Saudi Arabia and USA of its support while, maintaining close links with Iran. As events proved, that included transfer of nuclear technology.

In this context, it will be worthwhile to examine the role that China had played vis-à-vis Pakistan and Iran. China had remained a close political supporter and reliable supplier of military equipment to Pakistan since 1971 if not earlier. China also emerged as a major source of supply of arms to Iran during and after Iraq – Iran War. The supply included SCUD missiles that were used by Iran against Iraq during the war. One does not know when Iranians decision makers decided to acquire an independent nuclear enrichment capability that could be justified for peaceful purposes as also be upgraded for producing nuclear warheads. Once that decision was finally taken, Pakistan became an important partner in Iran's nuclear programme. While Pakistan's role is well documented, Iran's China links, direct or via Pakistan, in the context of acquisition of nuclear weapon technology as also delivery system has not been sufficiently probed.

Pak – Iran relations are going to be affected by Chinese policy in the region. China had developed links with Iran when it was isolated during Iraq – Iran war. After the disintegration of the USSR, China has sought to fill the vacuum in Central Asia. Pakistan and Iran can play a crucial role in the revival of the "Silk Route". It will project China as a major player and counterbalance not only Russia but also USA in this region. Energy is another sector that links China with Central Asia and

Iran. Pakistan can play an important role in transfer of energy resources via land from the energy rich region to energy consuming nation like China. This link will also reduce China's future dependency upon Russian energy resources. Thus, one can conceive of new great game being played by two major regional powers; Russia and China. Iran and Pakistan will most probably opt for China, especially when the West is seeking to militarily disengage itself from the region (Afghanistan and Iraq) by 2012-14. Thus, while analysing Pak – Iran relations, it will also be useful to look at it in the context of Chinese policy in this region. Afghanistan will be left with no option but to join that axis, a possible development that needs watching.

Pak – Iran strategic partnership, especially under the present regime in Iran, has further isolated India from Iran. India's vote against Iran on nuclear issue, its growing reluctance to obtain Iranian gas, as also gradual slowing down of its geostrategic communication links to Afghanistan and Central Asia via Iran, are matters of great concern. They have led to mutual misunderstanding. India must take steps to remove that misunderstanding before Iran commits itself fully to the new Iran – Pak – China axis. Does India have a credible interlocutor who can be entrusted with quiet diplomacy, a role that P N Haksar had played in assuring the Shah of India's good intentions in 1973-74? It is time that we search for some interlocutors not only for Iran but also for others as well to enable decision makers to quietly smoothen the rough edges and remove misconceptions in bilateral relations, especially with states that are of strategic importance for India.

Professor K.R.Singh*

---

* Formerly Director, National Security Programme and Gulf Studies Programme, School of I nternational Studies (JNU); Chair , Mari time Studies and R esearch (University of Calicut).

Preface

Iran, which extends its nationalism and national identity, back to the centuries even before the advent of Islam, is among the great empires of the ancient world. The most important festival in Iran today, for example, is *Nowruz*, the pre-Islamic Persian New Year, when rather than going to mosques, Iranians follow the tradition of lighting bonfires to welcome the Spring. Iran being located at the juncture of West Asia, Central Asia and South Asia and endowed with a huge hydro-carbon resource has always been strategically considered a pivotal country. Because of its national aspirations and vital geo-politics, in modern times, it has been in focus in international affairs. The popular resistance to imperialism, as evidenced in a mass uprising by the Iranians against the concessions to the British in 1892, was a major event not only in Iran's nationalistic politics but also in strategic affairs. Iran became the centre of the century-long 'Great Game', the original spy-versus-spy, in which the British and Russian agents manoeuvred in Iran for Queen and the Tsar. Successive shahs managed deftly to keep Iran independent. After the discovery of Iranian oil in 1905 (followed quickly by the British Navy's decision to convert coal to oil-fueled ships) and the outbreak of the Cold War after the Second World War, Iran's strategic position bolstered in the region and Iran's nationalism had been identified by the popular uprisings seen in 1951-53 during the Mossaddeq era and in 1978-1979 Islamic Revolution.

Pakistan, on the other hand, is a fairly new creation. In fact, it started to exist as a state in August 1947, only when it got separated from the Indian subcontinent. All its histories and politics earlier were, therefore, identified with the British India. Hence both Iran and Pakistan represent two distinct patterns of political systems and navigating their relationship is a very difficult task indeed. However, new developments between them in recent years have created salutary interest among scholars of international relations to focus on their long term relationship. So the present study has been undertaken to discuss various facets of this relationship in a long term perspective by analyzing them under various phases.

The period from 1947 to 2010 has been chosen to analyse this relationship, particularly from an Iranian angle, in the context of different ruling systems such as monarchy and theocracy so as to understand the overall state pattern of Iranian foreign policy. The first chapter is a short introduction that traces the Iranian independence in a modern state system. The second chapter covers the entire gamut of Iranian foreign policy towards Pakistan followed under a monarchial system. It covers the period from 1947 to 1978. The third chapter is an analysis of the relationship of the Islamic Republic of Iran with Pakistan from 1979 to 1989. The fourth chapter is an in-depth study that covers the period from 1990 till the current regime to understand the tone and tenor of a modified theocratic foreign policy pursued under various Iranian Presidents and its approach towards Pakistan. The fifth chapter is the conclusion that is a total assessment of the relationship between the two states with some fresh and prognostic thoughts.

Main Arguments of the Paper

The paper argues that Iran's relation with Pakistan, over the years, has been very friendly with minor frictions at times. Domestic, Regional and international factors have played a decisive role in shaping Iran's foreign policies towards Pakistan. However, it is the domestic politics which has always played a predominant role in shaping Iran's foreign policy. It is also arguable that Iran's foreign policy has been strategic in nature. In recent years, this nature has its reflections when followed towards Pakistan. The paper further argues that such a strategic policy, in due course, may include other important regional players such as China in maximizing Iran's national interests. The paper explores that if such a relationship is not properly addressed through brinkmanship either by India, which is a very important regional player or US which is the most important, extra-regional power, it may spell problems for the regional security of Asia. In fact, the important developments that are now shaping Iran-Pakistan relations will pose a series of challenges to the regional as well as global security.

Why Iran-Pakistan Relations and why now?

Iran's relation with Pakistan and *vice versa* has been a fascinating subject of study in international relations. In recent years, because of complexities and incongruities involved in this relationship, it has attained wide attention and has become a major area of focus for scholars, particularly Asian. Since I am an Indian having an avid and abiding interest on the developments of Iran and as there is no full length study currently available on the subject, the present attempt is a relevant and timely one, albeit, in a shorter version, to fill that gap.

Scope of the Paper:

The scope of the paper is confined to relations between Iran and Pakistan, although a sporadic mention about Iran-India relations and Iran-US relations has found some space. It is mainly strategic in nature and the broad period covered is from 1947 till date. The said period is so chosen because the bilateral relationship between Iran and Pakistan can be analyzed over a long period of time within a set of complex international state system of modern history.

Acknowledgements

At the outset, I must express my deep obligation to USI, especially to Lt. Gen P. K. Singh (Director, USI), Maj. Gen PJS Sandhu (Deputy Director and Editor, USI) and Col. V. K. Singh (Deputy Director, Administration, USI), for providing me the fellowship in Centre for Strategic Studies and Simulation, USI to work on a project; "CRAFTING A STRATEGIC ENGAGEMENT WITH IRAN", of which the current book is only a part.

The initial impetus to work on a full-length study on "Iran-Pakistan Relations" has come from Prof. K R Singh, who has provided a foreword for this book. When it was prepared I solicited his comments. He, with his exceptional academic and gnomic style, not only read the entire manuscript, more than once, but also provided very valuable inputs. His suggestions not only illustrated his exceptional knowledge of Iran and his love for Iranian people, but also became the mental springboard in reshaping my thoughts on Iranian history and politics, especially on Iran-Pakistan Relations, a topic attempted by few scholars on a full-length basis. I would like to acknowledge my special gratitude to Prof. K R Singh, for his deep motivation and encouragement in writing this book.

In fact, the idea of a monograph grew after I presented a paper on Iran-Pakistan Relations in April 2009. The occasion was graced by Amb. K C Singh, Secretary, MEA (Retd.), who was not only chairing the presentation but also happened to be my supervisor on the project: "Crafting a Strategic Engagement with Iran". His inputs, not only then but also now, has been highly crucial and benefited me a lot in bringing out a monograph like this. I owe a deep sense of gratefulness to Amb. K C Singh for his constant help and support.

I am truly indebted to Cmde. M R Khan, Senior Fellow, Centre for Airpower Studies (CAPS), Delhi, who had not only provided very valuable inputs as a special discussant when the paper was being discussed in USI but also had given an elaborate list of critical comments on the monograph as an examiner. I have not only re-analysed all his comments in a deeper way but also incorporated them only to discover that the book has been highly enriched.

I am also very grateful to Dr. Meena Singh Roy, Research Fellow, Institute for Defence Studies and Analyses (IDSA), for her crucial inputs that she had provided as a second specialist on the paper when the paper was being presented in USI.

While undertaking the writing of this paper, I have been immensely benefited, at various stages, by my interactions with a number of experts on various issues. They include Prof. Girijesh Pant, Vice Chancellor, Doon University, Dehradun, Prof. Gulshan Dietl, Chairperson, Centre for West Asian Studies, JNU, Prof. A.K.Pasha, Director, Gulf Studies Programme, JNU, Prof. Sujit Dutta, Gandhi Chair, Nelson Mandela Centre for Peace and Conflict Resolution, Jamia Millia Islamia, Prof. GVC Naidu, School of International Studies, JNU, Dr. Vijay Sakhuja, Director of Research, Indian Council of World Affairs, New Delhi, Dr. P.K. Ghosh, Senior Research Fellow, Observer Research Foundation, New Delhi, Captain Alok Bansal, Executive Director, National Maritime Foundation, New Delhi, Dr. Bhashyam Kasturi, Senior Fellow, Nehru Memorial Museum and Library, Teen Murti House, New Delhi, Dr. Smruti Pattanaik, Research fellow, Institute for Defence Studies and Analyses (IDSA), New Delhi and Dr. Sumita Kumar, Senior Research Associate, Institute for Defence Studies and Analyses (IDSA). I would like to record my thanks to all of them.

Dr. Sarmistha Pattanayak, Dr. Poonam Mann and Dr. Tanya Mohan deserve special appreciation for the academic inputs that they have provided on various chapters of the monograph even through e-mail.

I am also indebted to my colleagues in Centre for Strategic Studies and Simulation (CS-3), particularly to Tuhin, Archana and Dhananjay, for the support that they have provided at various walks of this book. I deeply value their friendship beyond its academic merits.

Last, but by no means the least, I would like to express my special thanks to Mukesh Kumar Jha who extended all help in accessing very valuable materials that were available in IDSA library.

Nobody except me, however, can be blamed for any mistake, if committed, in this work.

1

INTRODUCTION

Iran, although ruled under a monarch, enjoyed state freedom from foreign occupation, particularly after the Second World War, around 1946-1947. It was a fact that modern Iran's independence was a product of the Anglo-Russian rivalry that had preoccupied the Iranian state since the nineteenth century and continued into the twentieth century. Hence, an attempt must be made here to understand this rivalry, commonly known in history as the 'Great Game'[1] ("a term usually attributed to Arthur Conolly, an intelligence officer of the British East India Company's Sixth Bengal Light Cavalry and was introduced into mainstream consciousness by the British novelist Rudyard Kipling in his novel *Kim)* so as to understand the rise and growth of modern Iran's independence and the evolution of its foreign policy.

Great Powers and Iran in the Nineteenth Century

Britain, with regard to Iran, had a two plank policy: one related to the securlty of the jewel of its Crown, India and maintenance of the British position in Iran was regarded as vital to the safety of India; the second was *vis a vis* Russia.

Great Britain's interests in Iran were inextricably bound up with the British imperial interests in India. Whether it was the Persian, the Central Asian, or the Persian Gulf question that occupied the minds of British policy makers, the paramount consideration was the maintenance of British imperial interests in India. Because of this pre-eminent objective, the British government was basically committed to a policy of the status quo in Iran. Pursuance of this policy often required advancing British influence, but on the whole this influence was sought primarily in order to counter the

Russian threat to the independence of Iran. Great Britain needed Iran as a buffer state, and perhaps the stronger the buffer the better. But its course of influence building in Iran was jeopardized by the competing countermoves of Iran's proximate neighbor, Czarist Russia. It became very much concerned about the Russian efforts and ambitions to gain control over Iran.

Russia, in the first half of the nineteenth century, was busy in expanding its southern borders at the cost of Iranian territories. It had not only annexed Georgia and many other territories of Iran but had also vastly expanded its southern borders at the cost of the Qajar empire in Iran. Russian conquests were confirmed even by forced treaties such as the Treaty of Gulistan (1813) and the Treaty of Turkumanchai (1828). Iran's territories have remained so till today as Russia and the Soviet Union has been its northern neighbor or big brother. The British who looked askance of the Russian developments into Iran's northern territories also occupied Herat which was a part of Iranian territory. The British interests in Herat were linked to Great Britain's imperial interests in India. Herat was regarded as the starting point of routes to Kabul and Qandahar from which ran natural lines of invasion into India.

In the second half of the nineteenth century, the Anglo-Russian rivalry became a furious economic competition in Iran. Iran, in 1872, decided to put into the hands of a single man the entire responsibility for Iran's economic and industrial development. To this end, it granted to Baron Julius Reuter, a naturalized British subject, an all-encompassing economic concession for a period of seventy years. This concession was, in Lord Curzon's words, "the most extraordinary surrender of the entire industrial resources" of the country. The grant of such a gigantic monopoly to a British national aroused severe Russian opposition. Russia claimed that the grant had completely repudiated Iran's claim to adhere to the principle of equilibrium between the great powers. After the Reuter concessions, in 1888, Great Britain obtained a concession for the establishment of regular navigation on the Karun river. Russia feared British penetration and commercial competition in northern Iran. This apprehension was intensified when Great Britain attempted to acquire a concession for the construction of a railway from the upper Karun river to Tehran. Russia therefore, decided to prevent the construction of this or any other railway in Iran. This marked another phase of Anglo-Russian rivalry for the control of Iran.

Great game and Iran in Twentieth Century

During the last few years of the nineteenth century and the first few years of the twentieth century, Anglo-Russian rivalry also became a dominant feature in Iranian affairs because of many factors. First, the then British Government in India feared that Russian influence might penetrate to the province of Sistan, the eastern province of Iran contiguous to then Indian frontier. Lord Curzon, in his famous dispatch of September 21, 1899, accorded Sistan great significance. By reason of its geographical position in relation both to northern Khorasan, to western Afghanistan, to British Baluchistan, and to the Persian Gulf, Sistan, he said, is of no small strategical importance. It "is the present meeting point of the advanced pioneers of British and Russian influence." "The Government of India could not contemplate without dismay the prospect of Russian neighbourhood in Eastern and Southern Persia."[2]

Second, British trade, in the Persian Gulf, had acquired almost a monopoly of the foreign commerce of the Gulf ports. Indians had settled in considerable numbers at Lengah, Bandar Abbas, Bushire etc. Foreign imports and exports passed through the hands of these settlers. The many Anglo-Indian companies maintained a merchant steamer service between Karachi and Persian Gulf. British communication interests in the Persian Gulf were equally significant. Hence maintenance of the British position in the Persian Gulf in general and Iran in particular was regarded very important.

Third, the Russians, in the closing years of the nineteenth century, had also attempted to gain a foothold in the southern Iranian area of the Persian Gulf, but had failed. In the following years Russian warships toured the Gulf and Consulates, were established at Basra, Bushire, and Bandar Abbas. These attempts by the Russians to gain influence in the Persian Gulf had alarmed the British. Lord Lansdowne, the then British Foreign Secretary, in one of the important declarations, had emphasized:

> "We should protect and promote British trade in the Persian Gulf. We should regard the establishment of a naval base or a fortified port in the Persian Gulf by any other power as a very grave menace to British interests, and we should certainly resist it by all the means at our disposal."[3]

But soon circumstances began to change primarily because Germany was determined to challenge Great Britain's rule of the seas. Berlin had launched its major program of naval rearmament in the Persian Gulf. The "big navy" policy which was the pet child of Admiral von Tirpitz, Secretary of the Navy from 1897 to 1916, was supported by Kaiser Wilhelm. Germany was bent on penetration of the Persian Gulf, a policy that alarmed both Great Britain and Russia simultaneously. The ambitious Baghdad railway plan was designed to link the Persian Gulf with Konia, the terminal point of the German-controlled Anatolian railway. The concession for the railway was secured by Germany from Turkey in 1902, and in spite of British and Russian opposition the 200-kilometer stretch from Konia to Eregli was completed by the autumn of 1904. Thus, for the first time, Great Britain and Russia decided to cooperate for the sake of their great interests and official negotiations began in June 1906 and lasted for fifteen months, leading to the signing of the convention on August 31, 1907. Both Russia and Great Britain agreed to the Anglo-Russian convention of 1907 to maintain their interest in Iran.

1907 Convention and de facto partition of Iran:

 The provisions of the convention in regard to Iran amounted to *de facto* partition of the country, although the preamble contained the customary sanctimonious reference to the preservation of Iran's integrity and independence. After stating that Great Britain and Russia had mutually engaged to respect the integrity and independence of Iran, the convention went on to divide the country into spheres of influence. Because Anglo-Russian penetration of Iran had been accomplished chiefly by means of concessions, spheres of influence were allotted by reference to the concessions that the two powers allowed each other to obtain in certain areas.

The Russian zone was far larger and richer than the British and included Tehran, the capital city. This was a consequence of the fact that Russia, by the time of the convention, possessed far superior influence in Iran. Russia had already penetrated all the sphere allotted to it and was rapidly expanding into the regions beyond. Its political influence at Tehran was proverbial. The commercial value of the British zone was not its main attraction in 1907, although it was known to be a region of oil fields, the full richness of which became apparent only subsequently. Many Englishmen, although recognizing their inferior influence in Iran at the time, criticized the convention, particularly its clauses on Iran. Lord Curzon, for example, launched a full-dress attack upon it in the House of Lords. After calling it "the most far-reaching and the most important treaty which had been concluded by the British government during the past fifty years," he charged that "we had thrown away the efforts of our diplomacy and our trade for more than a century, and had handed over to Russia not only the trade route from Baghdad but also the important marts of Isfahan and Yazd."[4]

The Iranians could not understand that Great Britain and Russia were forced to sign this agreement by a communal fear of Germany's growing strength. A declaration by the two powers explaining that the purpose of the agreement was to prevent, not to provoke, an intervention did nothing to diminish the Persian uncertainties".[5] Further, while Britain maintained a quid pro quo, Russia remained busy in eying the northern borders of Iran for its lines of communication and transport, as well as its warm water ports, and later, its large petroleum reserves. The rapprochement gave Russia an unprecedented opportunity to intervene in Iran. It produced an entirely new set of conditions with which Iran had to contend until the Bolshevik Revolution.

Bolshevik Revolution and Iran

The Bolshevik Revolution in Russia and is post-Revolutionary approach created an entirely new scene for Iran. In fact, the Tsarist foreign policy, in its power projection over the Persian Gulf and beyond, posed far more serious and subtle problems to Iran than ever before. Iranian policy makers had now to deal with both the traditional methods of outright invasion and diplomatic pressure and penetration and the new methods of Communist subversion and propaganda. The imperialist policies of Tsarist Russia, which had long threatened British interest in Iran as a buffer for the defense of India, were now camouflaged, reinforced, and spurred into relentless action by the messianic tenets of Communist ideology.

The exact relationship between Soviet ideology and foreign policy, which has been the subject of much controversy, is beyond the scope of this study and should not detain us here. However, it is suffice to say that whatever this relationship may be, to Peter the Great and his successors the subjugation of Iran in order to control India had been a necessary step toward becoming "the true sovereign of the world". To Lenin and his comrades Soviet domination of Iran was to serve as a "vanguard of Revolution" in the East. K.M.Troianovsky, a Russian Communist, shed light on the Soviet aim of Iran when he declared:

"The ground for the revolution in Persia has been long prepared; it was prepared by the imperialists of England and Russia; only a jolt from outside is needed now, only initiative and determination are necessary. The Persian revolt can become the key to a general revolution. Owing to Persia's special geographical position and because of the significance of its liberation for the East, it must be conquered politically first of all. This precious key to revolutions in the East must be in our hands; at all costs Persia must be ours. Persia must belong to the Revolution.[6]

The element of revolutionary propaganda was, of course, present in both Soviet diplomatic and Communist party pronouncements. On December 5, 1917, the Council of People's Commissars of the Bolshevik regime issued an appeal addressed to the Muslims of Russia and East. This was a significant expression of the basic Soviet aims in the East, including Iran. Its bold, frank, and sweeping attack on imperialism was most ingratiating:

"Muslims of the East, Persians, Turks, Arabs and Hindus! All in whose lives and property, in whose freedom and native land the rapacious European plunderers have for centuries traded! We declare that the treaty for the partition of Persia is null and void. As soon as military operations cease, the armed forces will be withdrawn from Persia and the Persians will be guaranteed the right of free determination of their own destiny"[7]

Under the circumstances, the then Iranian premier, Vasuq al-Dawlah, who was feeling a threat to his position and had signed the Anglo-Persian agreement in 1919, justified to the Iranian people the presence of British forces in the country. The British government also justified the presence of its forces in Iranian soil primarily because they thought the Soviets were a greater menace than anybody else. "The integrity of Persia," Curzon had written, "must be registered as a cardinal precept of our imperial creed", but in the face of the Russian menace to the British imperial interests in India, the weakness and vulnerability of Iran were of great concern. In the chain of buffer states stretching between India and all European interference, Curzon regarded Iran as the weakest and the most vital link.[8]

However, as has been seen, the continuing attempt by the Russians during this time had resulted in an unsuccessful attempt in creating a satellite republic in Gilan, one of Iran's northern provinces, in 1920 that was of great concern not only to the Iranians but also to the British. This near crisis posed a double challenge to the Iranians: the problem of Marxism as an ideology and the threat of secession, and this twin threat persisted as a phobia among the Iranians. The problem reappeared with larger implications both during and immediately following the end of the Second World War.

Second World War and the Azerbaijan Crisis:

It may be noted that after the German invasion of Russia in June 1941 pushed Stalin into Churchill's arms, there was probably little chance that Iran would have avoided foreign occupation. Especially, since Reza Shah had built the Trans-Iranian Railway, which was finished in 1938 after nearly eleven years of work and a cost of $150,000,000 to $200,000,000, linking the Caspian Sea to the Persian Gulf,[9] Iran was simply too good a route to get supplies to the embattled Red Army for the allies not to occupy it.[10]

Suffice to add that Hitler's Blitzkrieg in the West and the East, on 22 June 1941, put the USSR in an extremely critical position. It became evident that she could only survive if the Allies came to her aid. While it was difficult for supplies to come from the north through Murmansk, it was impossible for them to come through the Mediterranean: Turkey had closed the Straits, Rommel and his Africa Korps were about to threaten Alexandria and the Germans were masters of Bulgaria and Greece. The Allies had, therefore, only one way in which they could safely help Russia and that was through the Persian Gulf. Iran became a strategic, if not tactical, area of prime importance.[11] Hence, on 23 August 1941, in Teheran, the Russian and British ambassadors were putting pressure on Iran to expel the German experts resident in Iran[12] and place the Trans-Iranian Railway (the railway was the most effective way of getting US supplies to the Soviet Union during the War) and Iranian port facilities entirely at their disposal.[13] When Reza Shah refused, Russian and British forces invaded the country. Some units of Reza Shah's army stood their ground, but most collapsed quickly. In less than two weeks it was all over. Mohammad Reza Shah, the twenty-one year old son of Reza Shah, was installed by the Allies on the Peacock Throne as Mohammad Reza Shah Pahlavi on 25 August 1941 and Reza Shah abdicated and was sent into exile to die a lonely death in South Africa in 1944.[14]

For Iranians the end of World War II had meant one thing: the end of occupation that they had hoped. The Americans remained firmly committed to that goal and reminded both the British and Soviets that Japan's formal surrender on 2 September 1945, set the deadline for full evacuation from Iran for 2 March 1946. Stalin, however, did not seem to share Washington's conviction that an independent Iran would be a positive development. Although his true intentions remain unknown, he seemed determined to see how much of Iran he might be able to annex or break up into smaller, less threatening satellite states. Hence he not only temporized stipulated withdrawal of the Red Army units from Iran but also had abetted in the creation of two Communist-dominated republics in a couple of Iranian provinces in the north. He had started his plans early during the War. Shortly after the Soviet troops entered Iran, Soviet Union sought to take advantage of Iran's wartime chaos in order to increase its influence. In October 1941, Stalin managed, through Muhammad Reza Shah Pahlavi, to release fifty-three Marxists who had been jailed by Reza Shah (father of Muhammad Reza Shah Pahlavi) in 1937, to form the Tudeh (Masses) Party. Although originally not Stalinists, they were persuaded to join the Soviet cause and thereafter received considerable Russian assistance. The Soviets encouraged the Tudeh to get out into the countryside and raise the political consciousness of the peasantry, who still accounted for two thirds of Iran's population in early 1940s. The Tudeh grew rapidly, sponsoring trade unions, rallying Iranian liberals, and recruiting disproportionately in northern Iran, where Soviet influence was the strongest. Simultaneously, Moscow worked hard to stir separatist sentiment among Iran's Azeri and Kurdish minorities, both of whose homelands conveniently had bordered the Soviet Union. The Russians freed almost all Azeri and Kurdish prisoners from Iran's jails, and provided them with the skills, funds, and motivation to go out and stir up the population. Moreover, the Russians sent large number of troops, technicians, officials, propagandists, labor agitators, and others to take over as much of Iranian civil society in the north of the country as they could, going so far as to establish a new, Soviet-controlled school system. In the autumn of 1944, the Shah made the situation worse by clumsily trying to rig the elections for the new Majles. The ensuing popular outrage galvanized a broad coalition of opposition groups against the Shah, including pro-British Majles deputies, tribal leaders, the upper class, middle-class intellectuals, bazaaris, right-wing nationalists, and the Tudeh. The Soviets saw this as a propitious moment and had the Tudeh make a broader grasp at power.

In the mean time, on August 2, 1945, the new "Big Three" — Truman, Attlee, and Stalin—met at Potsdam to decide the fate of the postwar world.

This time, the conference declaration stated that all Allied troops must be withdrawn from Tehran right away and the rest in stages from the remainder of the country. But Soviet actions suggested a different intention. Immediately after the conference, the Russian press launched a massive campaign against Iran, supporting the creation of separate Azerbaijani and Kurdish states. The Central Committee of the Communist Party of the Soviet Union instructed the local Communist commander in Azerbaijan to begin preparatory work to form a national autonomous Azerbaijan district with broad powers within the Iranian state at the same time to develop a separatist movement in the provinces of Gilan, Mazandaran, Gorgan and Khurasan.[15] While the Tudeh had made great strides, many Iranians viewed it with suspicion due to a perception of foreign sponsorship. In Iran, the Communists and many sympathetic leftists coalesced into a new organization with a fresher face –a group founded at the direct instructions of the Soviet government as part of its plan to take over Iranian Azerbaijan. In 1945, these Democrats swept to power in Azerbaijan's provincial elections. Many had spent time in the Soviet Union, and almost all were sympathetic to Soviet aims. With Soviet troops backing the Democrats, Iranian authorities had little power to intercede as Azerbaijan declared its autonomy, mandated that Azeri rather than Persian be taught in schools, and took over local military posts. By 1946, Iranian Azerbaijan was flying its own flag and issuing both currency and postage stamps.[16]

Soviet tentacles also extended into Iranian Kurdistan. While Iranian history is replete with examples of separatism, no area in modern times has been so susceptible to ethnic separatism and violence than Iranian Kurdistan. Iranian Kurds, like other communities at Iran's periphery, lost much of their local autonomy relative to the central state during the first decades of Reza Shah's rule. The Shah's efforts to pacify the periphery, modernize and strengthen the army, smash tribal confederation, and build new roads had all taken their toll on the power of local Kurdish sheikhs. But, the Allied invasion and the subsequent expulsion of the Shah in 1941 had shifted the balance of power. And the Soviet Union moved to fill and exploit the power vacuum, sponsoring and nurturing separatist movements. In 1942, a group of Kurdish intellectuals formed a leftist nationalist group called the Komala. Centered in the small town of Mahabad, the Komala established cells in a number of Kurdish towns, spreading a separatist message among a fertile constituency. When Iranian government troops were sent to get control of the unruly province, they were blocked by Soviet forces—still deployed in Iran and showing no sign of leaving. On 22 January 1946, the Kurds followed suit and proclaimed a Kurdish People's Republic with Mahabad as its capital and also immediately signed a mutual defense pact with Azerbaijan.[17]

Iran thus had the honor of becoming the arena for the first crisis of the Cold War, and it fell to the United States to solve the problem.

Cold War and Iran's Independence

The Truman administration was not looking for a fight with the Russians so soon after the end of the war, but they were also determined to get Stalin out of Iran. For the moment, they urged Iranian nationalists to bring the matter before the new United Nations Security Council and await the expected withdrawal of Soviet troops in February. But the withdrawal never came; the last American soldier left Iran on January 1, 1946. The British moved more slowly (they may have been waiting to see what the Russians would do), but they were in the process of leaving and announced that all of their troops would be out by March 1. Not only did the Russians not say anything about leaving, but they began to promote the propaganda that the people of Tehran also demanded liberation. This series of events convinced Washington that it needed to step up the pressure on Moscow. President Truman alerted American military forces to be ready to deploy to Iran, including three combat divisions in Austria awaiting their return to the United States. These moves seem to have finally gotten the Russians' attention, and on March 24, Moscow announced that all Soviet troops would be withdrawn. In May 1946, Soviet forces finally pulled out of Iran. Shortly after the Soviet withdrawal, Tehran and Washington concluded agreements for additional military assistance and substantial military assistance.[18] The event which is commonly known in history as the Azerbaijan Crisis and often reckoned as the harbinger of the Cold War is considered as the facilitator of independence for Iran. And the crisis weighed on the psyches of the Iranian people who interpreted the events and Communism as potential threats to the territorial integrity of the state, their social system, and to their regime security.[19] Similarly after the World War II, by November 1945, Soviet Union had not only influenced a large chunk of northern Iranians but also set up puppet separatist regimes in Iranian Azerbaijan and Kurdistan, and seemed determined to detach them effectively from Tehran's control and to force Iran to grant Moscow major oil concessions. It was said that Iran enjoyed freedom not because of its innate strength but because of the balance of powers in Iran's northern and southern flanks during 1945-6. So an independent Iran's foreign relations (under the Shah) evolved against this situation.

Pakistan's Independence

Pakistan commenced its relations with Iran after it achieved independence, a democratic one, around the same time. Although it is beyond the scope of this work to discuss the origin of Pakistan's independence, a few facts must be mentioned so as to understand the evolution of its foreign policy towards Iran better.

The decolonization and partition of India resulted in the birth of Pakistan on 14 August 1947. Pakistan was the political outcome by a group of Muslims who prepared to defend their interests against the people of India during the British Raj with the eventual aim of claiming an independent territory. The standard bearer of the anti-colonial struggle in India, the Indian National Congress, was always opposed to what it termed 'Muslim communalism' by this group, since the Indian National Congress wanted to establish a plural nation where all religions could coexist. But the separatist attempt by the concerned Muslims had reached a climax in early 1940s. In May 1944, Gandhi did his best to convince Muhammad Ali Jinnah, the leader of these Muslim separatists, that there would be room for a Muslim community in an independent India, where it would enjoy considerable autonomy. But Jinnah could not be convinced. He became more resolute after his party, the Muslim League, fared well in the 1945 elections to various Indian legislatures in a process to attain self-government. Both the Indian National Congress and the Muslim League thereafter, in the context of India's independence, took steps that created bitter acrimony between the two and demanded separate states. The last chance of a united India was lost when the short-sighted leaders, especially Jawaharlal Nehru, failed to capitalize the proposals of Cabinet Mission sent out by the Attlee Government in May 1946, specifically intended to diffuse the crisis. Instead of a united India, it was divided and Pakistan was the result of such a division. It started to function as a democratic state and its foreign policy, and hence policy towards Iran, started to emerge with a specific focus on anti-India principle.

2

REZA SHAH PAHLAVI'S IRAN AND PAKISTAN
(1947-1978)

Internal Politics and Regime Insecurity of Reza Shah Pahlavi, 1947-53:

Iran's internal politics, traditionally, revolved around two factors: political leadership and army. These two variables often acted together though they could pose independent threats as well. Often the leadership assumed the primary role with the army acting as a useful tool. This was true about the *coup-d'etat* of Reza Khan (the father of Mohammad Reza Shah Pahlavi) in 1922, when he acquired power thanks to his 2000-strong Cossack Brigade.[20] Reza Shah Pahlavi's monarchial system, from the day of his accession, also was constantly being threatened by these two major actors. Not only were the military leaders suspect, suspicion also fell on politicians, some of whom were apparently loyal to the political system of Iran at that time. Cases of Qavam, Mossadeq and Amini have been highlighted by several scholars. Ahmad Qavam was the Iranian premier during the Azerbaijan Crisis of 1946 and was responsible for getting the Russian troops out of Iran in return for an oil agreement (which was subsequently rejected by the Iranian Majlis). The Shah thought that Qavam was flirting with the Russians in order to capture power. This was substantiated when Prime Minister Qavam, after the War (Second World War) rigged the 1946 Majles elections to remain in office. Unfortunately the party which he had built in opposition to the Shah and the British could not remain cohesive. There were simply too many groups with too many competing interests; once they were in power, their other differences emerged and pulled them apart.

Meanwhile, the Shah's power continued to grow as Iran's military power revived. Like his father, Mohammad Reza Shah retained a tight grip on the armed forces, lavishing them with resources and making sure to closely associate his own fortunes with those of the military. By 1949, he had rebuilt the Army to a strength of 120,000 men. Moreover, the huge boost in their morale after crushing the Azeri and Kurdish separatist movements in 1946 redounded to the benefit of the Shah, who had favored the military solution as opposed to Qavam's preferred political approach. The Shah's political fortunes were also bouyed by Qavam's problems, which allowed royalist Majles deputies to take a centrist position, playing the crucial swing vote in debates between the rightwing pro-British bloc and Qavam's left-of-center Democrats. In late 1947, the Shah fell strong enough to oust Qavam and install his own prime minister.

However, on 4 February 1949, the Shah narrowly survived an assassination attempt when five shots were fired at him at point blank range while he was attending an annual ceremony to commemorate the foundation of Tehran University.[21] The identity of the assassin was never accurately established although he was killed on the spot. However his papers showed that he worked for a religious newspaper (and therefore might have been a religious extremist), but he also paid dues to the journalists' union affiliated with the Tudeh Party. And it seems that not only was his assassin a religious fanatic, but a sympathizer of the Tudeh Party, who also had a mistress who was the daughter of a gardener at the British embassy in Tehran.[22] Whatever his true motives, the shah saw in the failed assassination attempt both a boon and an opportunity. The boon came from a huge boost to his popularity (similar to that of Nasser during early 1950s) for having survived the attack. The opportunity was to crack down hard on two major independent power centers in Iran, the Communists and the clergy. He declared martial law, introduced changes to the Constitution to allow him to dissolve the Majles, banned the Communist Tudeh Party, arrested many of its leaders, and arrested or deported a number of leading clergy who had been taking an active role in politics. In July, he went too far, attempting to fix the Majles elections, and when this became known, it triggered widespread opposition to his bid for autocracy. There was a deadlock to Iran's political process-the election to the Majles. The result was the formation of the National Front in October 1949. This was a broad coalition embracing much of Iranian political society, all of whom were now united in their desire to limit the designs of the young Shah and seek redress at the hands of the British.

The National Front managed to gather together reformist liberals of the new middle class and various religious groups, including some right-wing extremists. Among various Muslim groups, the most important group was led by Ayatollah Abolqasem Kashani. This group had coalesced its support to an eccentric figure, Muhammad Mosaddeq, who was an elder statesman of Iranian politics with a long record of opposing both the Pahlavis and the foreign oil companies. Since 1949 till 1953, Mosaddeq seemed to be the very embodiment of the said two causes that mattered most to the majority of the Iranian body politic. Consequently, his obsession with foreign interference in Iran (extreme even by the standard of the day) and his guiding assumption that the elimination of all foreign influence as a necessary precondition to Iranian political freedom, became even more firmly ingrained in the Iranian political ethos. For this Mosaddeq was consumed with foreign conspiracies to interfere in Iran, influence Iranian behavior, keep the country servile to Western interests, and remove independent-minded governments. That fixation on foreign plots provoked a foreign plot that sealed his fate by overthrowing him and paving the Shah for his autocracy. Although the Shah had enjoyed almost autocratic power thereafter, the threat of an army coup remained as long as the army remained under the control of strong leaders like General Razamara, who became a potential threat to Shah absolutism. The assassination of Razamara, it was said, was not deplored by the Shah; certainly it did remove the single most influential military leader.[23] But the danger of a coup remained. In January 1958, General Valiollah Qurani, who was regarded as the "Nasser of Iran",[24] was arrested and jailed on the charge that he sought to overthrow the regime.[25] So the Shah had perceived a continuous threat of internal political rivalry coupled with *coup d' etat* to the stability of his regime. It is amply clear that the Shah sought a closer relationship with the US not only out of fear of Communism and British Colonialism but also to sustain his own regime legitimacy. He frequently mentioned these threats and was quick to dismiss the internal problems as a result of the plots created as much by the Communists as by the British. He sought American aid not only for domestic economic reasons but also to save his monarchy. Relations with Pakistan started in such a footing of Iran's internal atmosphere when the young Shah was rebuilding his strength.

Reza Shah Pahlavi showed keen interest in maintaining a formal relationship with Pakistan soon after the creation of Pakistan. It stemmed from two important geo-political considerations. First, an Islamic state of Pakistan became the immediate neighbour and could be treated as a buffer against India that was still considered a part of the British colonial power; and second, an integrated and separate state of Pakistan was of singular importance to Iran because of the ethno-linguistic problems that Iran was facing. It was observed that Iran showed considerable political sympathy to Pakistan's overtures from the very beginning and was the first country to extend recognition to Pakistan's independence in 1947.[26] Its diplomatic mission began to function in Karachi in the same year.[27] It also appointed its first ambassador to Pakistan in May 1948 and established full-fledged diplomatic relations with Pakistan as early as May 1948.[28] Remarkably Iran became the first country that advocated Pakistan's admission to the UN.[29]

Pakistan's abiding love for Iran arises from the fact that not only is Iran an immediate neighbor but also the mother of Pakistani culture.[30] Pakistan, right from its birth, in pursuit of its ideology and consolidation of its legitimacy, capitalized on the new relationship. It sought friends to malign India. Muslim countries to its west were its first arena of activity. Thus Iran was an obvious choice. Pakistan perceived Iran as an important neighbour with which people of Pakistan shared common faith and history. Pakistan believed that maintenance of cordial ties with Iran was important for its own economic prosperity and security. Iran, therefore, became a key element in Pakistan's foreign policy and the two countries reciprocated the friendly overtures.

To capitalize on this new relationship, the Quaid-i-Azam (of Pakistan) appointed Raja Ghazanfar Ali Khan as the first Pakistani envoy to Iran in May 1948.[31] The Pakistani Prime Minister, Liaqat Ali Khan, visited Iran in May 1949 and the Shah of Iran was the first head of the state to visit Pakistan in March 1950.[32] The two countries went further in signing a friendship treaty in the same month. It resulted in the reciprocal awarding of most-favoured nation (MFN) trade status.[33] They also signed a border demarcation treaty, a sound one, resolving some significant differences between them. In fact, the border question was a major issue of concern between Pakistan and Iran existing immediately after Pakistan's creation. After its creation Pakistan automatically inherited about 590 miles of a common frontier with Iran. The boundary, which was partially demarcated, runs from Koh-i-Malik, the tri-junction of Afghanistan, Iran and Pakistan, to Gwadar Bay, in the Arabian Sea. Pakistan's border with Iran is also an imperial British legacy. Some parts of Baluchistan had also been under Iranian suzerainty before the advent of the British Raj. Britain, after conquering Baluchistan, entered into border agreements with Iran in 1871,

1896 and 1905. But the Baluch-Irani boundary remained largely demarcated. There were two reasons for this: First, as the border was less troublesome than the Baluchistan-Afghanistan frontier, the British Government showed little interest in a proper demarcation of the boundary. Secondly, with the extension of British influence over Siestan and Persian Baluchistan in 1907, the Perso-Baluch border alignment lost much of its political significance. During the Second World War, Siestan and Persian Baluchistan, there was none the less some Iranian territory-including the town of Zahidan, the terminus of the railway from Quetta-which did come under Pakistani control. As a result of confusion about boundaries existing in 1947-49, some border clashes occurred. But neither Pakistan nor Iran ever made any public statements on border issues. More serious was the fact that some of the later clashes took place in the mid-fifties. Hence, in 1955, on Pakistan's suggestion, the two countries agreed to submit their boundary problem to arbitration if direct negotiations between them failed to produce the agreement. Accordingly, in July 1955 the two governments agreed to appoint a joint commission. The Commission was charged with the task of adjudging the Safavid dispute and rectifying the 'Goldsmid line'. By 30 October 1956 it was reported that complete demarcation of their boundaries had been reached. By October 1957, the Pakistani cabinet had completed considerations of the draft agreement which was formally signed on 6 February 1958. On 17 September 1959, an agreement was signed at Tehran to provide facilities to the nationals of Pakistan and Iran in the spheres of residence, occupation, ownership and transfer of property and commercial assets to either country.[34] The final protocol on the Pakistan-Iran Boundary Accord was exchanged on 31 August 1960. On this occasion an Iranian writer claimed that the 945-Kilometer-long Iran-Pakistan border was demarcated in a record time of eight months, whereas the 2,000-Kilometre long Iran-Soviet boundary took seven years to complete.[35]

In the meantime, President Ayub Khan described, in a statement to the Iranian Senate in 1959, said, "Our two nations are no strangers to each other, our friendship is nothing new. Our links are steeped in history. We share the same faith and are heirs to a common cultural heritage. Your language and literature has for centuries been a source of inspiration to our people. We have drunk deep at the fountain of the Iranian culture and it has left indelible marks on our every day life. . . . Historically we have been one nation in the past, geographically we have a common border and ethnologically we are of the same stock."[36] He also described the

Pakistan-Iran accord as a landmark in the history of Pakistan-Iran relations.[37]

Iran-Pakistan bond and the regional factors (during 1950s, 60s, and mid-1970s)

(a) Regional organisations and Cold War system

After the Second World War, the tremendous increase in Middle East oil production made the area more important. Geographically the region lie astride the routes to South Asia and Africa. In war time its control by Russia would outflank NATO, and its use by the Western countries would provide a useful springboard for an assault on the USSR over a wide front. Britain, who had traditionally barred the Russian advance towards India, was too weak after the Second World War to checkmate Russian moves single-handed. In 1951-2 there was talks first about the establishment of a Middle East Command sponsored by the US, UK, France, and Turkey, and then of a Middle East Defence Organisation (MEDO). Both schemes, however, failed, principally because they did not attract the Near Eastern countries of the region on whose membership these arrangements were to be based. Iran and Egypt had unsettled disputes with Britain about oil and the Suez base respectively. And the Arab states too were preoccupied with their conflict with Israel to think of participating in an alliance under Western leadership to contain Soviet Union. During 1954 the question of Middle East defence grew in urgency because Britain abandoned the Suez Base in October and the Anglo-Iraqi treaty of 1930 was about to expire. A mutual defence assistance agreement between Iraq and USA was signed in April 1954 and the Iraqi premier, Nuri es-Said Pasha, proposed that the moribund Arab League Collective Security Pact of 1950 be widened and strengthened. Thus the seeds of Baghdad Pact started to germinate and the Eisenhower Administration turned its attention to the security situation along the entire Northern Tier. John F. Dulles, the then Secretary of State, suggested the formation of a multilateral regional security arrangement that would help contain the Soviet Union.[38] Efforts in this direction culminated in the signing of the Baghdad Pact on 24 February 1955 by Turkey and Iraq, to join Great Britain and Pakistan on 05 April and 23 September respectively. Iran joined the Pact later on 3rd November.[39] It goes without saying that joining Baghdad Pact had brought Iran and Pakistan closer both politically and militarily, a development which India could not but look upon with considerable disquiet and trepidation. As Nehru told the Lok Sabha. "—— Baghdad Pact and SEATO—— have a direct effect upon us and naturally we have viewed them with suspicion and dislike".[40] It must be stated that it was only after Pakistan joined the Baghdad Pact that it could count on the support of Iran on the Kashmir issue both at the UN and outside. Iran also solicited Pakistan's support in its dispute with Iraq over Shatt-al-Arab waterway.[41]

Both Iran and Pakistan soon developed good relations to counter the common threat of Soviet expansionism and Eisenhower Doctrine facilitated it. Eisenhower Doctrine authorized the US President to aid non-Communist Middle East nations threatened by armed aggression from any country controlled by international communism as well as to use armed forces to assist any such nation or group of nations requesting assistance.[42] Both Iran and Pakistan maintained their membership in Baghdad Pact even when the pact was (later) restructured as the Central Treaty Organisation (CENTO) in 1959 after Iraq's post-revolution withdrawal. Inside the CENTO Iran and Pakistan shared identical approach in various procedural matters. It was only Pakistan and Iran who insisted that a unified command structure be imposed on the CENTO Army.[43] Probably the reason for this was that whereas the other CENTO members were also members of other defence alliances or had their independent or bi-lateral defence arrangements such was not the case with either Iran or Pakistan which were weak initially. Pakistan and Iran continued to collaborate under the auspices of the CENTO till their co-membership in CENTO was further modified in Regional Cooperation and Development (henceforward to be referred as RCD) which facilitated active cooperation between them during 1964-1979 until RCD was disbanded in 1979.[44]

The RCD, a tripartite agreement agreed among Iran, Pakistan and Turkey for non-political cooperation, born in 1964, was a regional arrangement. It was mainly the brain child of Ayoub Khan, the then President of Pakistan[45] Abdullah Riazi, the then Iranian Majles speaker, commenting on this organization, emphasized: "It would contribute to development of the member nations and to the cause of world peace".[46] Premier Hasan Ali Mansur also hailed the Iran-Pak- Turkey decision on closer cooperation as a great political, social, economic and cultural union of 150 million Muslims.[47] Iran and Pakistan were not limited to this association during that time. They soon identified themselves in the solidarity of the largest Islamic organization, the Organisation of Islamic Conference (OIC), by taking membership (which currently has 57 countries) in 1969 and thereby contributed to the feeling of 'Ummah (Islamic brotherhood)'.[48] The Iran-Pakistan bond of friendship was further accelerated by the regional factor of Afghanistan.

(b) Afghanistan Factor

Iran's Shah was very apprehensive of Communist expansion to the neighbouring region. The Republican coup in Afghanistan in July 1973, the secessionist movements in Baluchistan and Sind provinces of Pakistan have been documented by the Shah as the larger Soviet design to encircle Iran. Not only did the Shah take every effort to allay the Soviet fears from the region, he also ensured that his steps were well appreciated by the US. It was the time when the U.S. provided the Shah not only the little-known Tehran Research Reactor as part of a Cold War strategy, but also the weapons-grade uranium needed to power the facility to enable Iran as a powerful ally in the region against the Soviets. In fact, the Shah had decided that the only way to convince Washington to give him what he wanted was to make himself a key ally of the United States in the Cold War with Russia. The United States was opposed to Afghanistan-Soviet Union friendship, deployment of Soviet troops along the border of Afghanistan and Indo-Soviet treaty of friendship of 1971. Hence, the Shah preferred to be a strong U.S. ally and remained in the US camp as a matter of compulsion rather than choice. Iran found Pakistan a favourable ally following a similar strategy with US in the region.

When Pakistan won independence, Afghanistan was the only country in the world to oppose its membership in the United Nations.[49] Kabul took the plea that the Pakhtun and Baluch people inhabiting Baluchistan and the North-West Frontier Province (NWFP) bordering Afghanistan had not been given the right of self-determination and, as such, their territories were forcibly merged into Pakistan. This led to the Pakhtunistan problem, as successive Afghan governments publicly highlighted the rights of Pakhtuns and Baluch and demanded a separate homeland for the Pakhtun people. In 1961, Pakistan severed its diplomatic ties with Afghanistan over the question of "Pakhtunistan".[50] The problem had its reverberations for Iran's Shah because of its ethno-religious nature. Iran shared a common border with Afghanistan of more than 600 kilometers and the Balochi population was a commonly dispersed population among Iran, Afghanistan and Pakistan. Iran and Afghanistan were bound by historical ties.

Iranians had felt a strong kinship for Afghanistan historically, sometimes even considered it as an integral part of the Iranian homeland.

In modern Iran, even Reza Khan, the father of Reza Shah Pahlavi, had developed special relationship with Afghanistan. In 1921, both had concluded a comprehensive treaty of Friendship at Tehran. In November 1927, they had even signed a Treaty of Friendship and Security. In 1928, both Iran and Afghanistan went a step further in establishing the new bases of their relationship by signing two additional protocols.[51] Beyond the traditional bilateral relationship Iran had also invented ways to cultivate its relations with Afghanistan within the context of a regional grouping like the Saadabad Pact of 1937.[52] Hence there was sufficient reason for Iran to be worried about the crisis. The Shah of Iran, who maintained close relationship with Pakistan during this time, responded to this crisis by lending his good offices to bring about an eventual restoration of formal ties between Pakistan and Afghanistan. In May 1963 the Shah was instrumental in augmenting the direct negotiations between Pakistan and Afghanistan at Tehran and both Pakistan and Afghanistan agreed to re-establish diplomatic relations thereafter. It might be noted that, in July 1962, the Shah of Iran had floated the idea of a federation consisting of Iran, Afghanistan and Pakistan.[53] The Shah was prepared to accept to have a joint armed force and a common foreign policy as the minimum requirement for the confederation idea. Though the idea was probably mooted during the Shah visit to Afghanistan and Pakistan in the last week of July 1962, during his attempt at mediation on the Pakhtoon issue, it was broached for the first time in public on 6 August 1962 by Ayub Khan during his speech in Quetta.[54] Iran was willing to support an idea because it was searching for options vis a vis the USSR and the Arabs, especially in the light of the reduced American commitments during the Kennedy era. Iran was aware of the implications of such a union with economically weaker partners and was even prepared to bail them out financially too. The plan was good enough but the time was not ripe and it was dropped very soon.

One decade later, the Afghan government championed the cause of a Greater Baluchistan. Meanwhile, Iraq, in an effort to destabilize Iran, incited and supplied the Iranian Balochi population with weapons. In order to undercut Baluch irredentism, Iran, under the Shah, channeled weapons to, and helped construct bases for, the Pakistani armed forces. With this assistance, the Pakistani military waged campaigns to contain Baluch rebellions. In 1974, this military assistance was supplemented by a US$63 million grant tacked onto a previously awarded interest-free loan of US$580 million aimed at boosting the Balochi regional economy.[55] Thus Iran supported Pakistan's efforts both to suppress Baloch irredentism and to accommodate the Balochi population for its own national interests. The Afghanistan issue became a major factor in bringing both Pakistan and Iran together in the region. Reportedly Iran had offered US$2 billion in credit to Afghanistan during this period to assist Afghanistan in development of its infrastructure, also considered as a strategic step against Soviet expansion.[56]

The India Factor in Iran-Pak Relations

Pakistan, soon after its independence, sought to cultivate the friendship of its Muslim neighbors in order to strengthen itself against India and gain diplomatic support over various issues against India in the UN. In the late forties and fifties, this friendship was discernible with Iran providing diplomatic support to Pakistan over Kashmir, the most crucial test of a country's friendship in the eyes of Pakistan. In the Iranian Parliament Kashmir was discussed as an "inseparable part of Pakistan". Deputy Speaker, Sayed Ahmed Sarai said: We believe the decision of the Security Council should be binding, and the Kashmir issue settled through plebiscite under the auspices of United Nations. It is, however, regrettable that India on the one hand criticized even defence arrangements as envisaged in the Baghdad Pact and on the other hand believed in the outmoded maxim of might is right".[57]

In 1952 Iran volunteered to act as a mediator between India and Pakistan over the Kashmir issue but the tilt was clearly in Pakistan's favour. Iran's Foreign Minister Ardeshir Zahedi, for instance, declared that "Iran had been telling India to solve the Kashmir problem with Pakistan on the basis of self-determination". In 1956 when India showed her resentment over the mention of Kashmir issue in the Baghdad Pact Ministerial Communiqués, Iran did not pay any attention to India's protestations.[58]

The Shah made his first visit to India in February 1956 on India's invitation, just four months after Iran joined the Baghdad Pact. The Shah tried to impress upon the Indian leaders that his country's close ties with Pakistan were not directed against India and would not be at the cost of India's friendship. That no communiqué was issued at the conclusion of talks between Nehru and the Shah was an ample indication of the fact that the two leaders were on different political wavelengths and merely agreed to disagree. It must be underlined that Shah's relation with Pakistan, during this period, had also been shaped by an Indian inclination towards Egypt. In fact, Nehru's penchant for Nasser and the close relations between Nasser and Nehru prompted the Shah to move closer to Islam and Pakistan.

Nasser's crusade against monarchies had increased Shah sense of insecurity. The traditional Persian-Arab rivalries and suspicions and the sectarian divide between the Shiite Iran and the predominantly Sunni Arabs only accentuated the Shah fear of isolation and encirclement. The Shah tried to counter the threat of Arab radicalism as espoused by Nasser in two ways. First, he brought to make use of Islam as an ideology and second, he tried to cultivate non-Arab Muslim countries of the region such as Pakistan to counterbalance the regional forces. Though Shiite Islam was declared the state religion in Iran, the Shah of Iran was not a religious man in any sense of the term. Despite his political conservatism, the Shah was a modern and forward looking monarch. In fact, under the Shah, the emphasis in Iran was on the pre-Islamic Aryan civilization. His title "Aryamehr" meant "Light of the Aryans".[59] However, it was only Arab radicalism and India's pro- Nasser attitude that became a major force to bring Iran closer to Pakistan.

Strategic Depth and Iran-Pakistan Mutual Concerns

It may be mentioned that Iran-Pakistan relation was also shaped because of the strategic depth that Pakistan required during that time. In fact, Iran provided Pakistan the required strategic depth in the Indo-Pakistan wars of 1965 and 1971. During the Indo-Pak War of 1965, Iran considered the defence of Pakistan as its own defence. Abdur Rasul Azimi, the editor or Paigham-ilmroze clearly stated that "Iran came out to help Pakistan against 'Indian aggression' with full consciousness that it was helping the defense of its own country.[60]   In fact, immediately after the invasion of West Pakistan, Pakistan invoked CENTO. Though Britain and USA disclaimed responsibility under the pact, the two Muslim members, Iran and Turkey responded favourably to Pakistan's appeal for help.[61] Ironically during 1962-1971, Pakistan, a close friend and ally of Iran, was not only the closest ally of China but had also sought a close relationship with USSR.

Indo-Pak Wars of 1965 and 1971 and Iranian Responses

The Iranian foreign ministry, during the Indo-Pak War in 1965, reacted vehemently to the crossing of the international border near Lahore on September 6, 1965 by the Indian Armed Forces and described it "as an act of aggression committed by Indian forces against Pakistan".[62] Two days later, the Iranian Government not only condemned the "Indian aggression" but also promised every possible help to Pakistan. On 10 September the Iranian prime Minister along with the Prime Minister of Turkey expressed disapproval of the Indian attack on Pakistan.[63] At the UN General Assembly, the Iranian representative also argued in favour of a settlement "in accordance with the Security Council Resolutions and on the basis of the "principle of self-determination".[64] It was also reported later that there were deep consultations between the two nations at the highest level during the war and the Shah of Iran and President Ayub of Pakistan had exchanged important messages regarding all possible means of assistance. Though Iran could meet all of Pakistan's requirements because of a US objection, nonetheless, on the material side, its assistance consisted of jet fuel, gasoline, small arms and ammunition and medical supplies.[65] A number of nurses actually flew to Pakistan and served there.[66] YB Chavan, India's then Minister for Defence informed the Rajya Sabha on 2nd August 1965 that besides China, Iran and Turkey were also supplying arms to Pakistan.'[67] In response to earlier Indian statements, the Shah of Iran had accepted the fact that Iran was supplying arms to Pakistan. He had also justified his stand on the ground that had Iran not helped Pakistan with arms, Pakistan would have certainly jumped into the Chinese lap.[68] More importantly, according to him, the dismemberment of Pakistan, from a security angle, would have adversely affected the security of Iran.

Bangladesh Crisis and Iranian position:

The Bangladesh Crisis of 1971 had a marked influence upon Iran's South Asia Policy. The crisis began in March after the refusal of President Yahya Khan and Zulfikar Ali Bhutto, leader of the Pakistan People's Party (PPP), to allow the Awami League under the leadership of Sheikh Mujibur Rahman to fulfill its 6-point formula, that included granting of full internal autonomy to provinces of Pakistan under then new constitution that was to be framed. It should be remembered that the Awami League, that had secured 201 seats as against 99 seats of the PPP, had a strong base not only in East Pakistan but also in Baluchistan. By 26 March Yahya Khan proclaimed Martial Law in East Pakistan and unleashed a reign of terror. The same day, in response, the people of East Pakistan declared independence. A provisional government was formed on 28 March. Civil war broke out. Pakistan had stationed about 70,000 troops in East Pakistan who were equipped largely with American and Chinese weapons. The troops unleashed a reign of terror, atrocities, massacre and rape that led to massive exodus of population from East Pakistan to India. The people of

Bangladesh proclaimed the Democratic Republic of Bangladesh on 17 April 1971. Pakistan had full support of the USA, China and several Muslim states in its repressive policies in Bangladesh.

The growing seriousness of the Bangladesh Crisis had long-term internal and international implications for India. India was gradually isolated in international circle. Though the evolving Indo-Soviet relationship that culminated in signing the 20-year Indo-Soviet friendship treaty on 9 August 1971 had helped India to counterbalance the situation, India was facing some bitter criticism and opposition from the Muslim world especially Iran. Iran offered full political and diplomatic support to Pakistan. Within a month of the declaration of Martial Law in East Pakistan the Iranian Chief of Army Staff met President Yahya Khan. This was followed by a joint Iran-Pak air exercise, *Irpak,* during which a few Iranian F-5 and F-86 jets were reportedly transferred to Pakistan.[69] It was reported that Iranian and Turkish pilots were flying either their own transport planes like C-130 or were flying Pakistani transport aircrafts and were helping Pakistan in ferrying troops from West to East Pakistan.[70] These pilots were reportedly filling the vacancies caused by the grounding of Bengali pilots after the crackdown in East Pakistan. Their services were covered up under the auspices of a joint tactical exercise by CENTO members. All this was done before the Bangladesh War of December 1971.

Apart from offering substantial military help to Pakistan during the Bangladesh Crisis, Iran also provided valuable political and diplomatic backing to Pakistan in its policy *vis a vis* Bangladesh. A spokesman of the Iranian Foreign Ministry in a statement to the Paris News Agency on 29 March 1971 said that Iran strongly advised all powers to refrain from interfering in the internal affairs of Pakistan.[71] The then Iranian Foreign Minister, Ardeshir Zahedi visited Islamabad on 26 June to deliver a special message from the Shah to Yahya Khan. Zahedi also denied that Iran intended to act as a mediator between India and Pakistan. The joint statement, issued at the end of Yahya Khan's Iran visit on 15 September, said that Iran and Pakistan pledged continued support to each other in matters of mutual interest. However, on 29 September the Shah, in an interview to *Le Figaro,* said that he had offered to mediate between India and Pakistan but India had rejected his offer. He added that Iran was "one hundred per cent with Pakistan".[72] One possible result of this total Iranian support was that Pakistan also supported Iranian occupation of the three islands in the Gulf.

Indo-Pak War of 1971 and Iranian response

Iran called Indian attack as an "aggression" and the Indian action as interference in Pakistan's domestic affairs. The Shah of Iran in an interview to a Paris paper openly acknowledged, "We are opposed to all interference in its (Pakistan's) internal affairs, we are hundred per cent behind Pakistan".[73] The Iranian Prime Minister also toed his ruler's line and said that "Pakistan was being subjected to violence and force".[74]

During the war, Iran rendered considerable help to Pakistan. Pakistani airline planes and other civilian aircraft were not only allowed to take shelter in Iran but also permitted to fly to bring essential supplies from other countries friendly to Pakistan. Iran offered modern fire-fighting equipment and experts when the oil tanks in Karachi were hit by the Indians. Iran also promptly met critical shortages of ammunition and aircraft. When Karachi was blockaded and otherwise rendered unusable Iran allowed strategic supplies like oil to be routed to Pakistan via the Iranian land routes. Iran also reportedly gave help in maritime air reconnaissance and also offered a fully equipped base military hospital. Undoubtedly this was very valuable assistance.[75]

The Bangladesh crisis and the 1971 war seems to have disturbed Iran's framework of its South Asia policy. In that framework Pakistan had an important role as a balancer not only *vis-a-vis* Afghanistan but also India. The break away of Bangladesh, the military defeat and the crisis of leadership in "West Pakistan during and after the 1971 war, gave a greater impetus to the centrifugal forces in West Pakistan. If these forces had been allowed to take their logical course Pakistan's role of a balancer in South Asia would have been jeopardized, and Iran's South Asia policy would have been seriously affected. The Shah explained his position on this matter in an interview to *Kahyan International*. Answering the question if the Indo-Pakistani war had altered the strategic situation in the region and whether the outcome of that war had any effect upon Iran's defence policies, he said:

> *If Pakistan remains a powerful country, strong and united, the danger will be less. But if what happened on the other side ever shook the unity of West Pakistan then very grave problems would be created for us. The same would be true from international point of view as well. The entire international scene would be changed.*[76]

The Shah was worried about the possible break-up of West Pakistan as late as 1974. In an interview to *Le Monde* of 24 June-1974, he said that he was merely worried when Bangladesh, broke away from Pakistan. But commenting upon the possible break-up of West Pakistan, he said that Iran would have considered intervening in any way to prevent an "intolerable" situation for Iran.

Thus Iranian policy towards Pakistan *vis a vis* South Asia immediately after 1971 was governed by the threat to Iran from the possible disintegration of West Pakistan. Pakhtoonistan and Baluchistan-would have become independent. Beside its repercussions on Iran's internal affairs it would have removed the strong balancer and even provide a convenient foothold to the USSR in the Indian Ocean next to Iran. Not only did Iran consider the threat of disintegration of Pakistan as real but many Iranian and other' scholars linked this threat of disintegration of Pakistan with the' threat of encirclement of Iran.

The Shah was so worried, about such a. development that he hinted in an interview to the *New York Times* that if Pakistan did break up, Iran might seize Baluchistan before anyone else could do so. It was also argued that the USSR had a large political and military presence in India, Afghanistan, Iraq, South Yemen and Somalia and operated a fairly large task-force in the Indian Ocean itself. Some circles in the Iranian capital had voiced the opinion that the July 1973 coup in Afghanistan did fit into a pattern of long-term Soviet plans for the encirclement of Iran. It should also be noted that the period 1971-73 witnessed an intense Arab-Israeli confrontation and the Soviet presence in the Eastern Mediterranean too was very substantial. All these factors were used to prove the encirclement theory and the Baluchistan movement was destined to play a crucial rote in projecting a serious threat to Iranian security under that theory.

No direct linkage between India and the Baluchi movement was established but the Iraqi and Soviet involvement was highlighted, especially after the involvement of the Iraqi embassy in Pakistan, in February 1973, in the transfer of Soviet arms allegedly to the Baluchi movement, was publicized. It is reported that the Iranian secret service tipped the Pakistanis about it. The whole episode was dramatized. The Iraqi ambassador to Pakistan, in a televised press conference, was asked about the contents of about seventy bags and crates that had recently arrived at the Iraqi embassy at Islamabad under diplomatic seal. The envoy replied that they contained books and literature. When those containers were opened it was revealed that they contained 300 submachine guns, 1000 spare magazines, over 65,000 rounds of ammunition, short-wave radio equipment and a manual in Russian language.[77] The equipment too was of Russian origin. It was easy to link this with the encirclement theory.

A conscious effort was made to-prove that India, Iraq and the USSR were engaged in the break-up of Pakistan and, therefore, were working together against the' interests of Iranian security. In short, the Shah suspected and feared the development of a Moscow-New Delhi-Kabul-Baghdad axis to the detriment of Iran's security and regional ambitions.[78] Consequently, the Shah made a public and unequivocal commitment to the territorial integrity of Pakistan in 1972 by stating that any attack on Pakistan would be considered an attack on Iran itself.[79]

Iran took a serious view of the developments in South Asia— creation of Bangladesh, defeat of Pakistan, growing trouble in Baluchistan and internal crisis in West Pakistan. Its responses to the changing environment in South Asia have to be studied in the context of Iran's basic policy of keeping Pakistan as a buffer and a balancer in South Asia. That accounted for full Iranian support to Pakistan during and shortly after the 1971 crisis. But while doing so Iran, wittingly or unwittingly, accepted Pakistan's enemies as its enemies, and therefore developed a conflictual relationship with India and Afghanistan. Thus Iran was dragged into the South Asian conflict as a partner of Pakistan. It not only harmed Iran's image as a friendly power which could hope to mediate or offer good offices in the resolution of regional disputes in South Asia, but also reduced the role of Pakistan as a buffer and a balancer by making Pakistan one end of the Pak-Iran axis that was seeking to influence South Asian politics. Though this change in Iran's South Asian politics was most welcome to Pakistan, it seriously affected the fundamentals of Iran's traditional South Asian politics under which Iran avoided getting directly entangled in South Asian problems.

The short-term reaction of Iran to events in the subcontinent was to give total support to Pakistan. No sooner had the 1971 war ended than the Shah of Iran paid a surprise visit to Pakistan on 8 January to meet Bhutto who had become the President of Pakistan. Bhutto made a return visit soon after. The two heads of state called for the withdrawal of Indian troops from all occupied Pakistani territories. It should be noted that Iran had not recognized Bangladesh and still accepted Bangladesh as a part of Pakistan. The Shah, however, cautioned Bhutto from taking any precipitate step that might further complicate the situation. The influential sister of the Shah, Princess Ashraf, visited Pakistani Baluchistan in May 1972. Unfortunately, that visit followed soon after the ransacking of the Iranian Culture Centre in Quetta by Balochi students, and the Quetta public meeting, that was attended by Bhutto and Princess Ashraf, ended abruptly following public disturbances. Iran also gave full support to Pakistan in its dispute with India over the question of about 90,000 prisoners of war and also on the question of recognition of Bangladesh. Iran refused to recognize Bangladesh till Pakistan had done so in February 1974.

The Iranian government continued to back Pakistani policies in Baluchistan and to support the territorial integrity of West Pakistan. This becomes clear from the statements of Premier Hoveyda and the Shah. The Shah, commenting on this subject during the visit of President Bhutto in May 1973, put the whole question very candidly. He said that whatever happened to Pakistan was of vital importance to Iran not only because both were Muslim nations but also because of Iranian national interests. But the Shah support was not unconditional. In his interview to NBC's TV programme on 30 July 1973, he said that Iran would not tolerate further disintegration of Pakistan. But he also added that Iran was not encouraging Pakistan to adopt an aggressive, hostile attitude towards India. It is interesting to note that this significant change in tone followed the visit of Indian Foreign Minister Sardar Swaran Singh to Tehran during 21-23 July 1973. That visit officially marked the beginning of the new detente between India and Iran. It is also reported that P.N. Haksar, a close confidante of Mrs. Indira Gandhi, had made several unpublicized "private" visits to Iran even earlier.

Iran's Military support to Pakistan

Besides political and diplomatic support Iran offered military aid to Pakistan to enable it to regain its lost strength and also to contain the revolt in Baluchistan. Sardar Ataullah Khan Mengal, former chief minister of Baluchistan, reportedly told a public meeting-on 5 June 1973 that Iran was helping Pakistan to build three military bases in Baluchistan. Ahmed Nawaz Bugti, another 'Baluchi' leader and an ex-minister, told the Urdu weekly from Lahore, *Zindagi,* that Iran was bearing the expenses of five divisions of the Pakistani army operating in Baluchistan. There were also allegations of direct Iranian participation in Baluchistan. The pro-National Awami Party's Urdu daily, *Shahbaz of Peshawar,* said that a large number of Iranian soldiers had been sent to Baluchistan via Zahedan to fight the Baluchi rebels. Air Marshal Asghar Khan, an important opposition leader in Pakistan, told a news conference on 25 September 1973 that Iranian helicopters were operating in Baluchistan. The Shah, in an interview to *Le Monde* on 24 June 1974, however, denied that Iranian troops were ever sent to Baluchistan to help fight against the rebels there.

Iran also offered direct military assistance to Pakistan. It was reported that Iran was going to transfer 50 old F-5 supersonic jet planes to Pakistan once it obtained the new F-5 planes that it had ordered. These Iranian planes would help replace the aging Sabre jets of Pakistan. There were also reports that several Patton tanks (M-47) were sent from Pakistan to Iran where they were not only up-gunned with a new 105 mm gun but also old patrol engines were replaced by more powerful diesel engines.[80] There were also reports that Iran will assist Pakistan in armaments once its other ultra-modern arms reach from the Unites States. In fact, after President Nixon's pledge in 1972 to allow Iran to purchase any nonnuclear arms it wanted, the shah went on a shopping spree. In 1972, he placed a $2 billion order for American jet fighters, helicopter gunships, and C-130 transport planes, and he followed up in subsequent years with orders for the most advanced US arms: F-14 fighters, AWACS control aircraft, Spruance-class destroyers, Phoenix and Maverick missiles, and a $500 million IBEX electronic surveillance system. US firms delivered more than $8 billion worth of arms between 1973-1978 although this was only one third of the actual orders. [81]

Attempts were also made to integrate the defence of Iran and Pakistan. It was reported that Iran and Pakistan had agreed to cooperate with each other in the field of defence. This understanding was reached during President Bhutto's visit to Iran in May 1973 though no overt announcement to that effect was made. The Shah had also promised, during Bhutto's visit, Iranian support against any secessionist movement in Pakistan. The semiofficial paper *ittilaat* of Tehran characterized the Shah's informal comment as a "defensive agreement" between Iran and Pakistan. Ramazani compared Iran's-Baluchistan and Pakistan policy with the Dhofar policy. "Like-Iran's military aid to Oman, this was another example of Iran's use of its newly acquired military capability toward the achievement of its basic objectives in the Persian Gulf area." Both Iran and Pakistan too began to develop a new interest in reviving the CENTO as a means to strengthen regional cooperation, especially between Iran and Pakistan, and also to justify more arms from, the USA. Iran also supported Pakistan financially and part of this economic support was supposed to be invested in Baluchistan. Bhutto announced in Quetta on 4 August 1974 that Iran had offered $63 million loan to Pakistan to boost the economy of Baluchistan. He added that it was in addition to the interest-free-loan of $580 million that had been offered earlier to set up textile and cement plants in Baluchistan. It was also reported that the Iranian and Pakistani participation in these projects was 51 per cent and 49 per cent respectively. Iranian and Pakistani Baluchistan were also linked by railroad.

Cooperation between Iran and Pakistan in the military-political area grew significantly. From 1972 to 1977 Pakistan not only concluded various military protocols but also provided access to its military installations and services to Iran.[82] Under the terms of these protocols Islamabad provided training facilities in Pakistani defence institutions for members of the armed forces of Iran. Bhutto's Iran policy not only cemented cultural ties, it also made Pakistan the recipient of much needed economic and financial assistance. The assistance can be divided into three categories. In the matter of general purpose programmes, Pakistan received funds from Iran amounting to US $730.00 million. In the second category, project assistance, Pakistan received an amount of US$75.00 million. In the final category, Relief Grants, Pakistan received an amount of US$2.70 million.[83] During 1974-76, Iran agreed to grant Pakistan two loans, one for $580 million and another for $150 million, and several loans for the construction of industrial and other projects.

Undoubtedly all these developments helped Iran to safeguard, its security interests in its eastern frontier, at least in the short run. But in that process it strengthened the powers of Bhutto and further weakened the democratic structure of Pakistan that had been shocked by the events of 1971. The result was that the Bhutto regime was overthrown by a military coup d'etat in 1977. An internally divided and politically weak Pakistan could never protect Iran's eastern flank. But that logic could probably have never appealed to the Shah and his advisers who looked at security from a short-term and basically military point of view.

As seen earlier, Pakistan's initial reaction to the events of 1971 had brought Iran and Pakistan too close for comfort. It had also put Iran into a conflictual relationship with India which the former had always tried to avoid. Thus, if Iran had to revert back to its traditional policy in South Asia, and play the role of a mediator, it had to work out a detente with India and Afghanistan. Such a thing was difficult because of the belief in the encroachment theory. It, however, took time for India to convince Iran about the wrong hypothesis on which that theory was based, especially as far as it concerned South Asia, that India (and Afghanistan) had a vested interest in the break-up of Pakistan and that they were working in cooperation with Iraq and the USSR to bring about an independent Baluchistan. Quiet diplomacy on the part of India finally convinced Iran about the wrong hypothesis on which that theory was based. There were also several other factors that helped in this Indo-Iranian detente. By the middle of 1973 this trend towards Indo-Iranian detente had become, visible, and by 1974 their relations bad reverted to the pre-1971 level.

Pakistan, in searching for multiple options in its confrontation with India, had pursued a policy that could be construed to be antagonistic to Iran's security interest. In the sixties, Pakistan's close friendships with the USSR and especially with China were not in the best interest of Iran. In the seventies Iran took serious objection to Pakistan's close ties with the Arab countries in the Gulf and with Libya. Despite the common policies like membership of the CENTO, RCD, Islamic Bloc etc., Pakistan could not create a binding link between itself and Iran. Pakistani emphasis upon friendly relations with Iran is only perfunctorily noticed by the latter. The growing rift between Iran and Pakistan was noted by some Pakistani experts. Iran's tense relations with its Arab neighbours on the Gulf until 1975 caused it to adopt a cautious attitude towards Pakistan's policy of systematically cultivating these Arab states, especially the UAE and Saudi Arabia. Thus, the fact that Pakistan could not remain a dependent variable also influenced Iran to respond favourably to India's friendly overtures in 1973.

For strategic as well as sentimental reasons Pakistan focused its attention on the Islamic states. Iran was one of the first countries which Z.A. Bhutto visited in his capacity as the head of state in January 1972. President Bhutto called this visit "a journey among brothers".[84] In the post-war years, Iran's whole hearted support for Pakistan in the 93000 prisoners of war dispute was discernible from this angle. During this period, high level visits from both sides were also reported. During 1972-1977, the Shah of Iran and Bhutto met fifteen times, a record unequalled by any other exchange.[85]

Iran's attitude and actions in both the Indo-Pak wars show that though Iran was pro-Pakistan, it was hesitant in totally spoiling its relations with India. Iran tried again and again to make it clear that it did not want the dismemberment of Pakistan because that would have adversely affected the domestic stability and security of Iran. The Kurds in Iran would be encouraged to rise up against the Iranian government and thus jeopardize the security of Iran. Suffice to add that the Pakistani government, in a public statement issued later on May 8, 1973, stated: "Collaboration with Iran is essential to Pakistan's defence strategy because Pakistan lacks strategic depth and the only country which can and has provided this depth is Iran".

Iran, during the Shah, wanted not only to be a regional power but also to be a global power. He often spoke about his ambitions to be an Indian Ocean power. The Shah's military build-up and heavy reliance on USA including arms purchase, his anticommunist rhetoric and his regional policy towards Baluchistan and Bangladesh vis-à-vis Pakistan falls in that category. Ironically Iran faced major security threats not only from inside but also from outside in achieving that goal. The perception of 'encirclement' was also a major security threat. He feared that the independence of Pakistani Baluchistan would have a comparable effect upon the people of Iranian Baluchistan. If Baluchistan did break away from Pakistan it would seriously affect Iranian strategic perspective in South Asia. Pakistan would no longer prove to be a balancer. It would not be a buffer either. The USSR, with a friendly Afghanistan and a friendly Baluchistan would not have only a land corridor to the Indian Ocean but would be able to have naval facilities in the Makaran Coast, just off the Strait of Hormuz. This would complete the encirclement of Iran because, according to the proponents of this theory, Iran was already encircled from the north by USSR, and the west by Iraq. The Dhofar movement was already posing a serious threat to Iran and the Baluchi movement would have completed the circle. The Shah was so worried about such a development that he even hinted in an interview to the *New York Times* that if Pakistan did break up, Iran might seize Baluchistan before anyone else could do so. It was also argued that the USSR had a large political and military presence not only in neighbouring Afghanistan and Iraq but also in South Yemen, and India and a fair amount of Soviet task forces were present in the Indian Ocean as well which could entrap Iran any time it wish. Iran's policy towards Bangladesh *vis a vis* Pakistan also is interpreted in a similar fashion. The Shah was so obsessed with the integration of Pakistan that he even did not recognize Bangladesh as a separate nation and accepted it as a part of Pakistan. The shah continued to back Pakistani policies and even commented that Iran would not close its eyes to any further secessionist movement in Pakistan.

Barring a few minor differences when Iran was disappointed due to a Pakistani vote in favour of Bahrain's membership in the UNESCO in September 1966, implicitly recognizing Bahrain's sovereign status which was not acceptable to Iran[86] and similarly the Shah's grandiose scheme for the eventual emergence of an Indian Ocean Economic Community and his desire for close collaboration between the navies of India and Iran to keep the Indian Ocean free from outside encroachment which was not a good project for Pakistan to accept it,[87] Iran-Pakistan relationship, during the period under review, was excellent.

3

REVOLUTIONARY IRAN AND PAKISTAN (1979-1989) AND RISE AND GROWTH OF IRAN-PAK NUCLEAR RELATIONS

In the late 1970s, dramatic political changes took place at national, regional and global level. A military coup in Pakistan that brought Gen Zia to power in 1977 also witnessed revolutionary agitation and upheaval in Iran that overthrew the regime of Reza Shah Pahlavi in 1979. These important political events at the national level were succeeded by the Soviet invasion of Afghanistan in 1979 and the out break of Iran-Iraq war in 1980 at the regional and global levels.

With General Zia's accession to power, Pakistan's militant *Jama'at-i-Islami* appeared to have found the first champion of its long-standing goal to impose more strict observance of Islam on the country. It was argued that General Zia's Islamisation campaign had aimed primarily to build and maintain support for his martial law regime. Whatever his true motives might have been, the consequences of his efforts were far-reaching. In fact, they emboldened the *Jama'at*, who expected and demanded the swift and complete institutionalization of Hanafi jurisprudence or Sunni interpretation of Quranic law. Further, the kind of Islamisation process in Pakistan vaguely conceptualized by Zia and stridently advocated by the *Jama'at*, frightened the Shi'i minority, which comprised about one-fifth of the population. Thus, Pakistan's Islamisation process under Zia contributed directly to the heightening of Sunni-Shi'i tensions.[88] The Iranian Revolution, which occurred within two years of General Zia's accession to power, not only unleashed new social forces but also earned Iran the wrath of a super power. It disturbed the strategic balance in the region.[89] It was such an important political event in the region that it became a catalyst of Shi'i's political disaffection in Pakistan. Iran, a revolutionary State, emerged as a cardinal challenger to the *status quo* of not only the Persian Gulf states but also to many other Sunni Islamic states and USA in the region.

After the regime of Reza Shah Pahlavi was toppled in Iran, Islamabad became the first country to recognize the new Iranian provisional government.[90] Remarkably, both Pakistan and Iran withdrew from the CENTO in the same year. For Iran, ending its formal association with CENTO marked the transformation of Iran-US relations. But, in case of Pakistan, termination of its membership in the organisation held no such symbolic significance. Unlike Iran-US relations, the relation between Pakistan and United States remained warm. Further, Pakistan was more concerned with the sub-continental balance with India while Iran was worried for its Gulf status as well as for the antipathy created by the US supported Gulf regimes. But both the countries were concerned about the common threat posed by the then Soviet Union. The Iranian and Pakistani governments were sensitive not only to the possibility of a Soviet invasion, but also to Soviet encouragement of separatist challenges to their respective regimes. In recognition of their common predicaments, the fragile ethnic composition of their respective populations and vulnerability of their national economies, neither regime has appeared willing to exploit nor to contribute further to the other's weakening. Tolerance of Pakistan's military and non-military cooperation with the Arab states of the Gulf can be said to have reflected, in part, Iran's understanding of the importance of such ties to Pakistan's economic well-being.[91] However two important events, which occurred simultaneously during this time, had also stored a lot in themselves, to shape the bilateral relations between Iran and Pakistan. The first was the hostage crisis in Iran that started in November 1979 and continued till January 1981 and the second was the Soviet intervention in Afghanistan which commenced in December 1979 and remained there until February 1989 when its troops were finally withdrawn.

Hostage Crisis

On November 4, 1979, an angry mob of some 300 to 500 Iranian students laid siege to the American Embassy in Teheran, Iran, to capture and hold hostage 66 U.S. citizens and diplomats. Although women and African-

Americans were released a short time later, 51 hostages remained imprisoned for 444 days with another individual released midway because of illness through the ordeal. The students claimed that they occupied the American Embassy to avert another U.S.-orchestrated coup to restore the Shah to power. Suspicions among Iranians arose after the U.S. admitted the Shah for medical treatment in October 1979. On April 7, 1980, the United States broke diplomatic relations with Iran, and on April 24, 1981, the Swiss Government assumed representation of U.S. interests in Tehran. Iranian affairs in the United States were represented by the Embassy of Pakistan, in the Iranian Interests Section, in Washington, DC.[92]

The hostage crisis became one of the defining moments in Iran-US relations. While Iran has been perceived by the Americans as an "elephant in the living room of US policy"[93] ever since, the Iranians have also increasingly characterized the US as the "Great Satan, (an effective semantic tool by which Khomeini Islamized Marxist rhetoric against global capitalism and materialism)"[94] that has castigated Iran since long. While the hostage crisis left a terrible scar on the American psyche, the Iranians also felt that a symbolic action against the United States had helped the national unity of Iran and terminated a colonial relationship. Further, the Iranians justify that a new relationship had been inaugurated that had replaced an unfavourable model of relationship. However, the Iran-US relations have taken almost an antagonistic path thereafter. Iran has been busy in searching for a new foreign policy in the post-hostage crisis period. Although Pakistan had no such terrible experience with the US, its relation with Iran found a new focus because of the Soviet intervention in Afghanistan and Iran's new twist in its foreign policy followed thereafter.

Soviet Intervention and the Afghan Crisis

With the Soviet intervention in Afghanistan in December 1979, it changed further the geopolitics of the region where the US lost Iran and the Soviet Union gained Afghanistan. Although Pakistan, with the US help, started to emerge as the frontline state in the American-led coalition against Soviet intervention in Afghanistan, its relation with Iran started to flourish. The cooperation between Iran and Pakistan continued to flourish in all sectors.[95] Both Iran and Pakistan formed the Afghan Mujaheddin groups in their respective territories out of the refugees (who were pushed out of Afghanistan and had taken shelter both in Pakistan and Iran) to counter the Soviet threat. This mutual cooperation between Iran and Pakistan was further accelerated by the Iran-Iraq War of 1980-88. Although Pakistan, during this time, had become one of the most important allies of US and Iran —a staunch adversary, Pakistan supported Iran in its war against Iraq not only at an operational level but also economically, and otherwise, despite pressures not only from Saudi Arab but also from the US. It was reported later that when Vice-President Bush had visited Pakistan in 1984 during the war years, he had proposed a plan to Gen. Zia (during his talks at the Muree Government house) to help Pakistan train some Afghan Mujaheddin in Balochistan to destabilize Iran. But Zia had stoutly rejected the plan.[96]

It must be underlined that both Pakistan and Iran also took new initiatives in forming regional organisations. In 1985, the Economic Cooperation Organisation (ECO) was formed with Pakistan, Iran, and Turkey as its only members (Afghanistan, Azerbaijan, Kyrgyzstan, Tajikistan, Turkmenistan, and Uzbekistan joined only in 1992). Some politicians in the member nations see the ECO as a potential Muslim common market. In most of the concrete measures being taken by the ECO concerned the improvement of transportation and communications among the member nations, including the construction of a highway from Turkey to Pakistan through Iran.[97]

Iran-Pakistan bilateral relations were also very cordial during this period with high level visits from both sides at regular intervals. Mr. Zia ul Haq's visit to Iran in 1981 was followed by the visit of Mr. Agha Shahi, Foreign Minister of Pakistan, in the same year. An Iranian economic delegation visited Pakistan in early 1982 followed by the trip of Dr. Velayati, Foreign Minister of Iran, to Pakistan and signing of a cultural agreement in the same year. Mr Gulam Ishaq Khan, the then Commerce Minister of Pakistan, also visited Tehran in the same year and signing a long-term trade agreement.[98] In early 1983 Mr. Ghulam Ishaq Khan, Pakistan's Minister of Economy & Finance visited Iran reciprocated by the visit of Mr. Nouri, Iran's Interior Minister, to Pakistan. They signed a Memorandum of Understanding on Cooperation in Shipping.[99] In 1984 also, there was a visit by Pakistani Interior & Foreign Ministers to Iran which was reciprocated by Dr. Namazee, Iran's Minister of Economic Affairs & Finance, to Pakistan.

They also signed an agreement on formation of joint ministerial commission and a MOU on cooperation. In 1986, there was a historic visit of H.E. Ayatollah Khamenei', the then President of Iran, to Pakistan followed by the visit of Iran's Minister of Islamic Guidance and signing of the Cultural, Scientific & Technical Program at Islamabad.[100] This period and thereafter, through out the late 1980s, witnessed a huge expansion of Iran-Pakistan links in the defence field. Pakistan helped Iran to train its military personnel, supplied spare parts for the Iranian army's military equipment and machines, etc. They also signed a Defence Agreement in July 1989 which involved joint production of Pakistan-designed Al-Khalid Tanks.[101] It must be highlighted that during the mid-1980s two major and unrelated developments took place in international circle which had a profound impact on their bilateral relations and also on the affairs in international sphere. The first was the Iran Contra affair and the second was the Iran-Pakistan nuclear cooperation.

Iran-Contra Affair

In October and November 1986, two secret US Government operations were publicly exposed, potentially implicating Reagan Administration in illegal activities. These operations were the provision of assistance to the military activities of the Nicaraguan contra rebels during an October 1984 to October 1986 prohibition on such aid, and the sale of U.S. arms to Iran in contravention of stated U.S. policy and in possible violation of arms-export controls.[102] President Reagan and other senior U.S. officials had secretly facilitated the sale of arms to Iran, the subject of an arms embargo.[103]

Direct funding of the Contras insurgency had been made illegal through the Boland Amendment,[104] the name given to three U.S. legislative amendments between 1982 and 1984, all aimed at limiting US government assistance to the Contras militants. Senior officials of the Reagan administration decided to continue arming and training the Contras secretly and in violation of the law as enacted in the Boland Amendment.[105] It was planned that Israel would ship weapons to a relatively moderate, politically influential group of Iranians, and then the U.S. would resupply Israel and receive the Israeli payment. The Iranian recipients promised to do everything in their power to achieve the release of six U.S. hostages, who were being held by the Lebanese Shia Islamist group Hezbollah, who in turn were unknowingly connected to the Army of the Guardians of the Islamic Revolution. The plan was for Israel to ship weapons through an intermediary (identified as Manucher Ghorbanifar)[106] to a supposedly moderate, politically influential Iranian group opposed to the Ayatollah Khomeini. After the transaction, the U.S. would reimburse Israel with the same weapons, while receiving monetary benefits. The Israeli government required that the sale of arms meet high level approval from the United

States government, and when Robert McFarlane convinced them that the U.S. government approved the sale, Israel obliged by agreeing to sell the arms.[107] According to *The New York Times*, the United States supplied the following arms to Iran:[108]

- August 20, 1985.   -   96 TOW anti-tank missiles,

- September 14, 1985. -   408 more TOWs,

- November 24, 1985. -   18 Hawk anti-aircraft missiles,

- February 17, 1986.   -   500 TOWs,

- February 27, 1986.   -   500 TOWs,

- May 24, 1986.   -   508 TOWs, 240 Hawk spare parts,

- August 4, 1986.   -   More Hawk spares,

- October 28, 1986.   -   500 TOWs

Large modifications to the plan were devised by Lieutenant Colonel Oliver North of the National Security Council in late 1985, in which a portion of the proceeds from the weapon sales was diverted to fund anti-Sandinista and anti-communist rebels, or Contras, in Nicaragua.[109] Although it was claimed that President Ronald Reagan was not directly involved, handwritten notes taken by the then Defense Secretary, Caspar Weinberger, indicate that Reagan was well aware of potential hostages transfer with Iran, as well as the sale of Hawk and TOW missiles to "moderate elements" within that country.[110] Oliver North, one of the central figures in the affair, wrote in a book that "Ronald Reagan knew of and approved a great deal of what went on with both the Iranian initiative and private efforts on behalf of the contras and he received regular, detailed briefings on both." Mr. North also writes: "I have no doubt that he was told about the use of residuals for the contras, and that he approved it.[111] After the weapon sales were revealed in November 1986, Reagan also appeared on US national television and stated that the weapons transfer had indeed occurred, but that the United States did not trade arms for hostages.[112] On March 4, 1987, Reagan returned to the airwaves in a nationally televised address admitting that "what began as a strategic opening to Iran deteriorated, in its implementation, into trading arms for hostages."[113]

The affair, as President Reagan declared, began as an operation to improve U.S.-Iranian relations. President Reagan said, "My purpose was to send a signal to Iran that the United States was prepared to replace the animosity between the U.S. and Iran with a new relationship... At the same time we undertook this initiative, we made clear that Iran must oppose all forms of international terrorism as a condition of progress in our relationship."[114] But the real intention of Reagan was doubted because of its very nature of creating another potential faction in Iran opposed to Ayatollah Khomeini's faction. Hence the Iran-US relations could not be improved; rather the situation contributed further to the deterioration of a relationship already tinged with acrimonies. Surprisingly, this period had coincided with a new development, Iran-Pakistan nuclear relations, which had a profound impact not only on Iran-US relations but also on international relations.

Origin and Growth of Iran's Nuclear Program and Pakistan as an Alternative:

Before attempting Iran-Pakistan nuclear cooperation there is a pertinent need to trace the circumstances that has paved the way for and shaped such cooperation. Hence there is a need to trace the origin and growth of Iran's nuclear programme.

Iran has been pursuing nuclear weapons capability reminiscent since the time of the Shah. Iran's efforts to develop nuclear energy could be traced to 1957, in connection with a push from the Eisenhower administration to increase its military, economic and civilian assistance to Iran. On March 5 of that year, the two countries announced a "proposed agreement for cooperation in research in the peaceful uses of atomic energy" under the auspices of Eisenhower's Atoms for Peace program. The deal was intended to open doors for U.S. investment in Iran's civilian nuclear industries, such as health care and medicine. The plan also called for the U.S. Atomic Energy Commission to lease Iran up to 13.2 pounds of low-enriched uranium (LEU) for research purposes. Two years after the agreement was made public, Mohammed Reza Shah Pahlavi ordered the establishment of an institute at Tehran University-the Tehran Nuclear Research Center-and negotiated with the United States to supply a five-megawatt reactor. Over the next decade the United States provided nuclear fuel and equipment that Iran used to start up its research. Gary Samore, a senior arms control negotiator in the Clinton administration, later said that the cooperation was meant to assist Iran in developing nuclear energy while steering Tehran away from indigenous fuel-cycle research. On July 1, 1968, Iran signed the Nuclear Nonproliferation Treaty (NPT) on the day it opened for signature and ratified it in 1970. Six years later Iran completed its Safeguards Agreement with the International Atomic Energy Agency (IAEA).[115] By the early 1970s, the Shah approved plans to construct, with U.S. help, up to 23 nuclear power stations by 2000.[116] Following the Arab-Israeli War of October, 1973 when Iran refused to join the Arab oil embargo against the West and Israel and instead pleaded to use the situation to raise oil prices for using the money for modernization and to increase defense spending,[117] not only the US but also the European nations became ready to help Iran immensely. In March 1974, the Shah envisioned a time when the world's oil supply would run out, and declared, "Petroleum is a noble material, much too valuable to burn ... We envision producing, as soon as possible, 23 000 megawatts of electricity using nuclear plants."[118] In the same month itself, March 1974, he established the Atomic Energy Organization of Iran.

In 1975, US Secretary of State, Henry Kissinger, and Iranian Finance Minister, Hushang Ansari, signed an agreement allowing Iran to purchase eight reactors. That same year, the Western firms- France's Framatome and Germany's Kraftwerk Union AG-signed agreements with Iran for the construction of nuclear plants and supply of nuclear fuel.[119] It was reported that the Kraftwerk Union AG alone received $4 billion to $6 billion to build a nuclear power plant in Iran with a completion deadline of 1981. Iran also got the blessing of the US Atomic Energy Commission to receive the necessary fuel for two 1,200 megawatt –electric light water reactors and the promise to receive fuel that covered up to six additional reactors. In a related move that same year, the Massachusetts Institute of Technology reached a deal with Iran to train Iranian nuclear engineers. Kissinger issued a memo ordering a study of the Iranian deal in hopes of securing approval.[120]

In 1976, "President Gerald Ford signed a directive offering Tehran the chance to buy and operate a U.S.-built reprocessing facility for extracting plutonium from nuclear reactor fuel. The deal was for a complete 'nuclear fuel cycle'."[121] At the time, Richard Cheney was the White House Chief of Staff, and Donald Rumsfeld was the Secretary of Defense.[122] But the Shah had always been emphatic about the peaceful character of its nuclear energy. He even replied to a message sent by the then US President, Jimmy Carter, as: "I perfectly understand the particular attention which you pay to the question of nuclear energy, and fully realize the possible dangers and catastrophes which might result for mankind from an irresponsible attitude. In this field my wish is for Iran to put all her efforts towards the peaceful use of atomic energy. We shall continue to co-operate with all the nations of the world to attain this end."[123] While the Shah was on a marathon programme for Iran's nuclear power, he was surprisingly overthrown in 1979 by a Revolution. Iran's nuclear programme came to a standstill both because of a major setback that the US received during the revolution and the clerics who envisioned a different path for Iran.

But the Iraqi offensive against Iran during the Iran-Iraq War, especially the massive air strikes on ports and oil refineries in the Persian Gulf, showed the clerics that modern military technology, especially weapons of mass destruction, could make a decisive difference in war. The first few years of the Iran-Iraq War shocked the clerics into realizing the value of modern military technology. The War not only taught the Iranians that they should not expect help from other nations but also develop indigenous military, conventional and non-conventional technologies including nuclear technologies. The use of such technology would have deterred Iraq's initial aggression against the Islamic Republic. From the clerics' perspective, the Reagan Administration not only had opposed their aspirations but also allied with Iraqi Baa'th in an effort to defeat Iran. Had the Islamic Republic possessed nuclear weapons, the US might have thought twice about interjecting its Navy into the Persian Gulf and engaging Iranians.

Threats of Hostile Gulf Regimes and Pre-eminence of Israel and Pressing Iranian need for a Nuclear Power:

The fall of the "peacock throne" in early 1979 had the most effect in forcing a radical alteration of existing American policy. For one thing, the Iranian revolution in itself posed a threat to Gulf security. Saudi Arabia was not able to take over that role, even if it had been willing. Hence the Carter administration became convinced that the entire region was prey to increasing instability (thus the "arc of crisis" characterization). Hence the resultant US policy was a military linchpin and was known as Rapid Deployment Forces, or RDF introduced on 1 October 1979. Conceived as a force with a global orientation, the RDF soon focused its attention and planning in the Persian Gulf region. This narrowing of emphasis was precipitated by the Soviet invasion of Afghanistan on 26 December 1979. Subsequently an announcement was made commonly known in history as Carter Doctrine with respect to the Gulf region in January 1980 to protect the US interests in the Gulf region.

With evolving interpretations of the RDF's purpose and geographic orientation, the command structure of the RDF underwent repeated changes to Rapid Deployment Joint Task Force, or RDJTF. The decision to focus the attention of the RDJTF solely on the Middle East and Central Asia earned it a new name in 1983, U.S. Central Command (CENTCOM). However, the main purpose of the RDF remained the same, i.e. to protect the US interests in the Gulf. The US also signed a number of military agreements with the GCC countries which was created in May 1981 with the six Gulf-Arab states, namely, Saudi Arab, Kuwait, UAE, Qatar, Oman and Bahrain. The post-revolutionary phase was not only a reaction to the policies of US but also to the Gulf-Arab regimes in the region. Iran, under Imam Khomeini, not only perceived the US as a threat but also the regimes which were supportive of the US policy in the region. Hence Iran was operating in a region with forces which it considered as hostile.

The underlying reason for Iran's nuclear ambition was the perceived threat from regional powers, particularly Israel. The early 1980s had also compelled the clerics of Iran to revive their nuclear programme because of the renewed pre-eminence of Israel in the region as seen by the Lebanon War during 1982-1985. The 1982 Lebanon War called by Israel the "Operation Peace of the Galilee", and later colloquially also known in Israel as the First Lebanon War, began on 6 June 1982, when the Israel Defense Forces invaded southern Lebanon.

U.N. Secretary-General Kurt Waldheim noted: "a new cycle of violence has begun and has, in the past few weeks, steadily intensified." He further stated: "There have been heavy civilian casualties in Lebanon; there have been civilian casualties in Israel as well. I deeply deplore the extensive human suffering caused by these developments." The President of the U.N. Security Council, Ide Oumarou of Niger, expressed "deep concern at the extent of the loss of life and the scale of the destruction caused by the deplorable events that have been taking place for several days in Lebanon".[124]

Alexander Meigs Haig, Jr., the then Secretary of State and a former Army General and as well as the White House Chief of Staff under Presidents Richard Nixon and Gerald Ford was accused of "greenlighting" the Israeli Invasion of Lebanon in June 1982.[125] Although Haig denied these allegations, President Ronald Reagan's reaction during that time was that they would not apply any undue pressure on Israel to quit Lebanon as the Israeli presence in Lebanon might prove to be a catalyst for the disparate groups of Lebanon to make common cause against both Syrian and Israeli forces.[126]

However, during the crisis, Israel, after attacking the PLO, as well as Syrian, leftist and Muslim Lebanese forces, occupied southern Lebanon and eventually surrounded the PLO and elements of the Syrian army. Surrounded in West Beirut and subjected to heavy bombardment, the PLO forces and their allies negotiated passage from Lebanon with the aid of Special Envoy, Philip Habib. The war ended after three years in 1985, when Israel stabilized in the safety strap lengthwise the border but left a deep scar in the region that had prompted the Iranians to dispel the Israeli threat permanently. In recent times, Lebanon was found to be an ardent supporter of Iran's nuclear programme.

The clerics had realized that they had killed the goose which laid the golden egg by destroying the AEOI but soon decided to revive the organization with a new president who would resolve the issues with the German Kraftwerk Union in order to resume building the Bushehr nuclear power plant. The German firm refused, probably in response to pressure from the US. Nor did the French company Framatome agree on two 950 MW(e) reactors at Darkhovin, or on the construction of the Esfahan Nuclear Research Center. President Hashemi Rafsanjani recalled at that point that they realized that the West was not going to give sensitive technology to Iran and Iran had to search other for other suitable options. Hence, Iran turned to potential suppliers such as Pakistan, Argentina, Spain, Czechoslovakia, China, and the Soviet Union.[127] As events proved, Pakistan was a potential supplier thereafter.

Growth of Iran-Pakistan Nuclear Cooperation

It has been highlighted by various scholars that, during the Iran-Iraq War, the WMD programme of Iraq had created a lot of concerns for Iran. In fact, Iran found no strategic allies or even dependable friends, nor any international body which could lend support to it when Iraq launched devastating attacks. It was shortly after those attacks, Iran's nuclear research progamme which had gone dormant after the revolution, was revitalized.[128]

Noticeably Pakistan assisted Iran during this period in nuclear matters which the US suspected at a late stage.[129] It may be recalled that Iran had informed the IAEA in August 2003 that the decision to launch a nuclear enrichment programme had actually been taken in 1985.[130] It was a matter of public knowledge that Iran had discovered deposits of uranium estimated to exceed 5000 tons in 1985.[131] Iranian officials further described the programme as having three phases: the first phase from 1985 to 1997, the second phase from 1997 to 2002 and the third phase from 2002 onwards.[132] Media sources have also claimed that the period from 1986 to 1989 was one of extensive cooperation.[133] In fact, in 1986 Iran and Pakistan signed a nuclear cooperation agreement.[134] As per the agreement Pakistan offered to train Iranian nuclear scientists in return for financial support for its own nuclear programme.[135] The agreement specifically mentioned that 39 Iranian nuclear scientists and technicians would advance their skills in Pakistani nuclear facilities, reactors, and laboratories.[136] It was reported later that both countries had signed another agreement for joint development of nuclear weapons, under which Iran was to provide funding while Pakistan contributed through its expertise including training of Iran's nuclear physicists at the Pakistan Institute for Nuclear Science and Technology and the Khan Research Laboratories.[137] Suffice to add that the probe conducted by the International Atomic Energy Agency (IAEA) had concluded that there was "overwhelming assistance for Iran's nuclear programme by Pakistan as the source for crucial blueprints, technology and components for centrifuges".[138] B.S.A. Tahir, a Malaysian middleman of Sri Lankan origin, revealed to the Malaysian police that Abdul Qadeer Khan (A.Q.Khan), a Pakistani nuclear scientist, sold nuclear enrichment equipment to Iran. Mr. Tahir was asked by A.Q.Khan to supply centrifuges to Iran In 1994-95 and was paid US$ 3 million in return by an Iranian.[139] Before the probe began, Iran had also conceded to the IAEA that "it received crucial help from Pakistan".[140] In 1995, a news report mentioned that the US President Bill Clinton told Russian President, Boris Yeltsin, at a meeting in May 1994 that Iran was pursuing a nuclear weapon acquisition blueprint drawn up at least four years ago with the help of Pakistani officials.[141] It is now believed that Iran reached a deal with A.Q.Khan even much before 1987 for the supply of P-1 centrifuges while deliveries of designs and components began in late 1988 and early 1989.[142] Although not much is known about the exact timing of Pakistani assistance to Iran, based on various intelligence reports, it is perceived that the active cooperation had taken place during mid 1980s and late 1990s. This is also corroborated from the recent reports by the Washington Post which had quoted the IAEA officials familiar with Iran's nuclear activities which said that "Iran told inspectors that it acquired design plans for the centrifuges in 1987". Iran also accepted that Pakistan had cooperated in building a nuclear reactor in Iran in 1990.[143] The Pakistani cooperation to Iran's nuclear programme revolves around the lead role of A.Q.Khan in nuclear transfers. "Abdul Qadeer Khan," an investigative report by the *Los Angeles Times* stated, "a Pakistani nuclear scientist regarded by the US as a purveyor of nuclear secrets, has helped Iran for years". It also added: "even prior to 1989, Pakistani generals offered to sell Iran nuclear weapons technology".[144]

As far as Iran's enrichment programme is concerned, officials of the Atomic Energy Organisation of Iran (AEOI) stated that Iran had received drawings of the centrifuges through a foreign intermediary in 1986-87.[145] The IAEA reports that at Lavisan, the Physics Research Center attached to the Ministry of Defense, tried to acquire "dual use materials and equipment which have military applications... in the nuclear military area". Iran has not been able to explain these procurement attempts to the IAEA's satisfaction and has declined most of the IAEA's requests to interview relevant personnel. Most recently, analyses of environmental sample swipes of vacuum pumps acquired by the Physics Research Center show traces of highly enriched uranium (HEU). As with other HEU traces found in Iran, it is most likely due to contaminated equipment from Pakistan, but it raises the question about what kind of nuclear work was going on at the military facility at Lavisan. In 1987, Iran received a 15-page document from A.Q. Khan black market that described procedures for the reconversion and casting of uranium metal into hemispheres, which ElBaradei characterized as "related to the fabrication of nuclear weapons components." Iran's only reported response is that the black-market network provided the document at its own initiative, not in response to an Iranian request, and that Iran has done nothing with the document. The document raises many unanswered questions, including the role of the Iranian military in relation to the Pakistan connection.[146]

Despite extensive evidence about the links between Pakistan and Iran, Pakistan was not named as a source of international proliferation by the IAEA Director-General for quite some time. After the initial denials, the Pakistani government finally admitted that the former head of its nuclear programme, A.Q. Khan, gave Iran centrifuges for enriching uranium. But it continued to deny the involvement of the Pakistani government in any official capacity in such nuclear relations. In fact, Pakistan maintained a facade of innocence and even pardoned A.Q. Khan. But very few accept such a claim of the Pakistani government given the fact that the Pakistani military enjoys a very tight control over its nuclear weapons programme. Further, the various visits undertaken by A.Q.Khan to Iran and his schedules in Iranian military establishments and newer evidences could increasingly suggest the nuclear relation that existed between the Pakistani and Iranian governments when Zia was the President of Pakistan and Ayatollah Khomeini was the powerful cleric commanding Iran during that time.

Pakistani Motivations Behind the Cooperation

Even as revelations surfaced about Pakistan's transfer of nuclear technology to Iran, it was not immediately clear to many as to what the Pakistani motivations were in cooperating with Iran on this count. It does not appear to be in Pakistan's interest to provide a neighbouring country with nuclear technology which would affect its security interests. One would also expect Pakistan to be sensitive to Western attitudes regarding nuclear proliferation, especially since Iran has been viewed as a non proliferation concern in the United States for many years. At one level it would seem that the rationale for helping Iran could be explained by the importance given by the Pakistani leadership to strengthening the nuclear capability of a friendly Muslim country. Zulfikar Ali Bhutto was on record to establish Pakistan as a nuclear power following the detonation of an Indian nuclear device in 1974. Bhutto decried the international efforts aimed at preventing a Muslim country from acquiring such capability. Bhutto spoke emotionally about the need for an "Islamic Bomb". The "Islamic Bomb" was so called because it was alleged to be the product of Pakistan's technology and Middle Eastern finance in the 1970s.[147] Bhutto attached a great deal of importance to the possession of nuclear capability by the Islamic world, and this sentiment was also prevalent in General Zia-ul-Haq's pronouncements as well. In a July 1978 speech, President Zia outlined, "China, India, the USSR, and Israel in the Middle-East possess the atomic arm. No Muslim country has any. If Pakistan had such a weapon, it would reinforce the power of the Muslim world".[148] In an interview in 1986, he had reiterated: "It is our right to obtain nuclear technology. And when we acquire this technology, the Islamic world will possess it with us".[149] However, there is a certain section which is also critical about Zia's real intentions. Their argument has centred round the traditional Shiia-Sunni divide and the preferential treatment that the other leading Sunni states in the region such as Saudi Arabia would have received from Pakistan. But there was another angle also. Various sources had pointed out that General Zia perceived a major danger to his regime legitimacy after the Iranian Revolution of 1979 (i.e. Shiia radicalism to Sunni rulers). It was particularly so because General Zia had pursued an anti-Shiia Islamisation drive not only in Pakistan but also in neighbouring Afghanistan mostly during the 1970s. It was an open secret in Pakistan that Ayatollah Khomeini warned General Muhammad Zia ul-Haq –then military ruler of Pakistan-in no uncertain terms regarding the state behavior meted out to Shiias in Pakistan. At one point of time in 1980, Imam Khomeini had even told a Pakistani reporter, during an interview, that "if Zia continued to harass the Shiias, he (i.e. Khomeini) would do unto him (i.e. Zia) what he had done to Shah.[150]

No doubt the Iranian Revolution introduced a new form of sociopolitical organization, leadership, and activism to Shiism in Pakistani politics. The revolutionary elite in Tehran was eager to export revolution, and given the prevalence of Islamism in Pakistan's politics, viewed that country as a primary target. Iran initially approached the established (Sunni) Islamist parties of Pakistan, most notably the Jama'at. The Jama'at was impressed with the Iranian Revolution, but, as mentioned, had not endorsed its model of Islamist activism. Moreover, it soon became apparent that Iran was interested in more than its revolutionary experiences: through exporting the revolution, it intended to dominate the Islamist scene in Pakistan and beyond. Pakistan Islamists, the Jama'at in particular, viewed the Islamic Revolution as a positive step for Iranians and as a good omen for its own efforts in Pakistan.[151]   Soon after the revolution, zealous emissaries of the Islamic Republic –such as the first commander of the Revolutionary Guards, Mohsen Zamani, who had been trained in Lebanon and became Iran's ambassador to Pakistan, began to organize Shiia youth into militant organisations. This led to the emergence, in 1979 and subsequent, the growth of Islamia Student Organisation (ISO, a Twelver Shiia Organisation first formed in 1972) and the Tahrik-i-Nifaz-I Fiqh-I Ja'fariya (TNFJ, Movement for Preservation of Ja'fari Law), in 1979 renamed Tahrik-I Ja fariya Pakistan (TJP, Shia Movement of Pakistan), in Pakistan and the emergence among the Shiis of radical self-styled activists such as Aqa Murtaza Puya and charismatic "Khomeini-like" leaders, notably Allama Arif Hussaini. [152] The new organisations were inspired by the Iranian

Revolution, but had roots in the threat the Shia felt from the Zia regime and its Islamisation policies, which favored Sunni Islam. The name of the main organization, TNFI, bears testament to its defensive nature. The TNFJ was formed in April 1979 with the specific aim of protecting Shii interests in the emerging Islamic order. It was to be a pressure group responding to General Zia's Islamisation policies. Its architect was Mufti Ja'far Hussein, a senior Shiia *alim,* who had been appointed by General Zia to the Council of Islamic ideology to safeguard Shia interests.[153] Mufti Jafar was a moderate and was interested in organizing Shiias primarily to safeguard their communal interests. Still, the TNFJ soon set for itself the goal of formulating an Islamic constitution for Pakistan, based on Shia principle as expounded by Ayatollah Khomeini. The TNFJ gradually adopted a more aggressive and confrontational style. The inevitable transition to a more radical organization came with the death of Mufti Ja'far in 1983. In 1984 the organization split into traditionalist and radical camps. The division reflected tensions within the organization as to whether it should follow Mufti Ja'far's moderate approach or adopt a more revolutionary style. The latter approach won the day after Allama Arif Hussaini emerged as the TNFJ's leader in 1984. His charismatic revolutionary posturing consecrated the TNFJ's transformation into a militant body advocating radical sociopolitical activism with the goal of bringing about an Islamic revolution-modeled after that of Iran and following Khomeini's authority –in place of General Zia's Islamisation initiative.[154] This aim went beyond protecting Shiia interests in the existing order. It gave organized activism in Pakistan a new meaning and also defined the nature of anti-Shiia policies of the state and its allies among Sunni Islamist groupings. Hence it was quite discernible that General Zia had perceived a threat to his legitimacy and it was only opportune for him, when the regime of Ayatollah Khomeini had placed a request for the modern technology during the Iran-Iraq War, to capitalize on the situation.

While Pakistan's nuclear assistance to Iran can be traced to General Zia's time, Pakistan continued the assistance as a part of its state policy during successive regimes. Zia's successor, General Mirza Aslam Beg, felt that every nation had a right to possess nuclear technology and gave it due importance.[155] He not only supported Iran's attempts to acquire further nuclear technology but used this as a bargaining chip with the United States by threatening to transfer nuclear technology to Iran if Washington stopped arms sales to Pakistan. In 1989, Benazir Bhutto was approached by Iran with a proposition for a transfer of billions of dollars in exchange for nuclear weapons technology, which failed because of various reasons. But, during 1990, as reports have revealed, Iran had also received crucial help from Pakistan. In early 1991, there was motivation from Pakistan to help Iran in the nuclear arena involving various ruling elites from both sides such as General Asif Nawaz Beg, the former army chief of Pakistan, and President Rafsanjani of Iran and General Mohsen Rezai, head of the Iranian Revolutionary guard.[156] This involved the transfer of nuclear weapons technology by Pakistan in exchange for Iranian oil. However, this could not be materialized because of its exposure through Western intelligence. Although the nuclear relations between Iran and Pakistan have suffered some setbacks, no doubt, both the countries have pursued it continuously since it was started, presumably, during the mid-1980s. Iran has also lauded Pakistan's nuclear programme as a major achievement in the Islamic region. Kamal Kharrazi, former Foreign Minister of Iran, who visited Pakistan after Pakistan's nuclear break-out, was on record to greet the then Prime Minister, Nawaz Sharif, for the achievement, saying he had strengthened the confidence of the Muslim world.[157] Iran's top jurist, Ayatollah Mohammad Yazdi, during that time, had also publicly announced Pakistan's newfound nuclear capability as a way to achieve "equilibrium with Israel" at the tomb of Ayatollah Ruhollah Khomeini.[158]

Regional and International Concerns For Iran-Pakistan Nuclear Cooperation:

It is a fact that the Nuclear Nonproliferation Treaty (NPT), which Iran signed in 1974, allows Iran to build facilities involving all aspects of the nuclear fuel cycle, including enrichment, subject to international safeguards, more so because the U.S. continues to impose sanctions on the development of Iran's oil and gas sector (under the extra-territorial 'Iran Libya Sanctions Act').[159] It is also a fact that Iran will build nuclear weapon sooner or later. But there remains a regional concern particularly for India because of a serious *Jehadi* Terrorism that India faces not only within its territories but also on its borders both at northern, western and eastern flanks. In fact, the nuclear collaboration between Iran and Pakistan supports the hypothesis that Islamic states may forego divisions based on Shia and Sunni cultural ideologies and hence, a greater danger not only to India but also to both the West Asian and South Asian region as a whole.

It's an undeniable fact that Iran is a major player in both West Asia and greater Caucasus. A nuclear-armed Iran could transform the West Asian strategic landscape. But its role can be considered more as a potential balancer not only to many Arab Gulf states in military matters but also to Israel, a key ally of the US and also a symbol of the West in West Asia. But a few facts must be underlined. A nuclear Iran would tempt others in the region including Saudi Arabia to take the nuclear route. Hence there is a possibility that it would result in nuclear multipolarity in the region. It would also weaken deterrence in an already politically volatile region. There is also a possibility that Iran's nuclear material may fall into the wrong hands of Islamist terrorist groups or non-state actors. While the first two ways are almost certain and clear possibilities, there remains the third question whether Iran would be able check the fundamentalist groups in accessing its nuclear power.

India's concerns are just because of many reasons. Although India is not a part of the Non Proliferation Treaty (NPT), it has scrupulously followed all the basic obligations of an NPT member, resisting suggestions for nuclear cooperation that could have had adverse implications for international security.[160] At the same time, it can hardly be expected to ignore the potential risks arising from increased proliferation in its neighbourhood. India is uniquely placed in that it faces two nuclear adversaries- China and Pakistan, which has been augmenting its nuclear weapons capabilities with considerable help from China.[161] Any more addition to the nuclear club in Asia would further destabilize and complicate India's security environment. In such a context, nuclear proliferation related ties between Pakistan and Iran, and even China, is worrisome and can be very cautiously watched in Indian circle.

India has already suffered the adverse effect of collaboration between China and Pakistan in the nuclear and missile spheres, which included the transfer of the design of a nuclear warhead as well as other crucial technologies and components. With the changing international realities and India's expansion of the relations with major actors such as the US, Japan and Israel both in the region and in the international circle, India has to calibrate its policies in a different fashion. However, the global actors, so far, have given greater emphasis on scrutinizing Iran's clandestine nuclear transfers than checking such a proliferation axis. In fact, rather than identifying the extent of damage done by the proliferation networks and collaboration among states, the responsibility for proliferation is being assigned only to beneficiaries and not to their benefactors. As former Indian Foreign Secretary, Mr. Shyam Saran, very rightly puts it, "We see no reason why there should be an insistence on personal interviews with Iranian

Scientists but an exception granted to a man who has been accused of running a global "Nuclear Wal- Mart".[162] Demonstrating its sensitivity to the emerging challenges to nuclear non-proliferation regime, India voted twice in favour of the International Atomic Energy Agency's resolutions on Iran and expressed concerns about nuclear proliferation threats, particularly the type that Pakistan has demonstrated. However, the basic problem lies with an Islamic Bomb and now compounded by a proliferation axis tantamounting to threats to India's security in the neighbourhood.

As is evident, Iran-Pakistan relations, throughout the 1980s, have been very cordial and they have developed because of mutual interest even in a climate of hostile regional and international factors. This was a period when Iran had isolated not only many Gulf Sheikhdoms but also both the Super Powers. It was also the period when Iran was searching for friends who could support its nuclear programme. As events proved, it was none other than Pakistan who could provide the required support in the sensitive nuclear technology matters against all odds. Iran was supported by Pakistan, despite US pressure, in defence matters in her long-drawn war against Iraq. In fact, Iran had signed one of hers most elaborate defence agreements with Pakistan during the period under review. Although Pakistan, under Zia, was considered a frontline state of US in the region and Iran, under Ayatollah Khomeini and Ali Khamenei, was a staunch critic of the US, both Iran and Pakistan had accorded top priority to their national interests which had transcended the typical Shiia-Sunni framework. It was very clear from the support provided by Pakistan, a Sunni state, to Iran, which was a theocratic Shiia state, against Iraq-a regime ruled under a fellow Sunni, during the Iran-Iraq War. Hence it can be argued that both Iran and Pakistan, during this period, were pronounced friends rather than enemies, as was argued by many specialists earlier.

4

POST-COLD WAR IRAN AND PAKISTAN
(1990-2010)

During the 1990s, relations between Iran and Pakistan suffered some problems amidst new developments not only at national levels but also at the regional and global levels. Following the mysterious death of Zia-ul-Haq in 1988, the end of Iran-Iraq War in 1988, death of Ayatollah Khomeini in 1989, the withdrawal of Soviet troops from Afghanistan in 1989 and the rise of Taliban militias in Afghanistan in 1990-91 and the collapse of Soviet Union in 1991, there was a change in national, regional and global atmosphere.

In Iran, in 1989, Hashemi Rafsanjani was inaugurated as President. Rafsanjani was to serve for two terms in what became known as the 'era of reconstruction', to be followed by eight years of 'reform' under Khatami.[163] Both President Rafsanjani and his successor President Muhammad Khatami placed a strong emphasis on regional relations. But there was a rise of anti-Shi'ite terrorist activities in Pakistan mainly as the culmination of the Islamisation drive followed by General Zia ul-Haq during both 1970s and early 1980s.[164] Iran's Counsel General, Sadeq Ganji, was assassinated in Lahore in 1990 as a mark of this Shiia-Sunni rivalry. Pakistan had not only armed and trained these militants but also set them as army safeguarding Afghanistan. Soon both Iran and Pakistan supported opposite sides in the 1991-2001 Afghan Civil War.

With accusations from both sides during the Afghan Civil War, it is emphatic to note that high level visits were undertaken from both countries to strengthen not only the bilateral relation but also to diffuse the regional situation. The various high level visits included the visits by Prime Minister of Pakistan, Mr. Nawaz Sharif, to Tehran in 1991, 1992, 1993, the Pakistani President, Mr. Ghulam Ishaq Khan's visit to Tehran in 1991, Iranian

President, H.E. Mr. Hashemi Rafsanjani's visits to Islamabad in 1992, visit of Iranian Foreign Minister to Karachi in 1993, visits of Ms. Benazir Bhutto, Prime Minister of Pakistan, to Iran in 1993 and 1995, visit of Asif Ahmad Ali, the then Pakistani foreign Minister to Iran in 1994, visit of Iranian foreign Minister to Pakistan followed by Pakistani President, Mr. Farooq Ahmad Khan Leghari's visit to Iran in 1994, visit of Iran's Foreign Minister to Pakistan in 1996 and the visit of Mr. Aghazadeh, Iran's Petroleum Minister, to Pakistan in 1996; the visit of Mr. Sahibzada Yaqub Khan, Pakistan's Foreign Minister to Iran followed by the visit of Mr. Nawaz Sharif, Prime Minister of Pakistan, to Iran in 1997, visit by Dr. Kharrazi, Iran's Foreign Minister, to Pakistan in 1998, visit of the Pakistani Foreign Minister to Tehran; visit of Mr. Mohajerani, Iran's Minister of Culture and Islamic Guidance, to Pakistan in 1999, followed by two visits of General Pervez Musharraf to Tehran in 2000 and the visit by Dr. Rouhani, Secretary, Supreme National Security Council of Iran, to Pakistan, visit of Mr. Aminzadeh, Iran's Deputy Foreign Minister, to Pakistan, visit of Mr. Mousavi Lari, Iran's Interior Minister, to Pakistan and visit of Dr. Kharrazi, Minister for Foreign Affairs, to Pakistan in 2001.[165]

To minimize their bilateral differences, in one of the addresses given by Prime Minister Benazir Bhutto to the Iranian Majles on 8 November 1995, she had said: "Iran and Pakistan are not only two neighbouring but we are Muslim countries. Islam binds us together in a spiritual bond which others cannot share in the same manner. If Iran and Pakistan have raised their voice for the people of Kashmir, Palestine, Bosnia, Afghanistan it is because Islam binds upon us to speak the truth..... Iran and Pakistan seek peace wherever we see conflict.....My heart bleeds for the brave people of Afghanistan. A whole generation of young people have grown up in war, known only conflict, seen only sufferings. They fight each other for power. This is most unfortunate. We in Pakistan have decided not to give material or military assistance to any faction."[166] President Khatami's foreign minister, Kamal Kharrazi, had equally declared publicly in his first address to the UN General Assembly in 1997 that '[the] highest foreign policy priority ... is to strengthen trust and confidence and peace in our immediate neighborhood'[167]. However both Iran and Pakistan were at loggerheads during the Afghan Civil War.

During the civil war, Iran perceived the Taliban to be the creation of Pakistan and Saudi Arabia with US support. It was convinced that the Taliban was put together not just to contain the Iranian role in Afghan affairs, but more specifically to use it as a southbound route of the Central Asian Oil and Gas.[168] Pakistan supported the Pashtun Taliban while Iran supported the Tajik Northern Alliance. When the Taliban overran most of the country they sent shock waves in the region including Iran. This problem was subsequently compounded when the Taliban members captured the Afghan city of Mazar-e-Sharif in 1998. They not only massacred thousand of Hazara Shi'ites, but also assassinated scores of Iranian diplomats, straining Iran's bilateral ties with Pakistan. The killing of diplomatic and other personnel at Iran's Mission in Mazar-e-Sharif precipitated a grave crisis with the amassing of critical role in defusing the situation through the dispatch of special envoy, including the then Minister of State for Foreign Affairs of Pakistan, to Tehran. A fruitful meeting between the then Prime Minister Nawaz Sharif and President Khatami at the United Nations was also held in September 1998.[169] The two leaders decided that regular contacts between senior officials would promote understanding and improve relations further. The Foreign Secretary accordingly visited Tehran in the first week of January 1999 for bilateral consultations with his Iranian counterpart. During his visit he was also received by the Foreign Minster and the President. However, the continued sectarian violence in Pakistan became one of the most undesirable and contentious issues in the Iran-Pakistan relationship during that time. In order to contain the rising tension between Iran and Pakistan, Gen. Pervez Musharaf visited Iran in December 1999. His visit was also intended to secure legitimacy for his own regime. During his visit, Iranian President Mohammad Khatami described ties between Iran and Pakistan "as profound and unbreakable, noting the two countries' common cultural and Islamic foundations".[170]

India Factor in Iran-Pak Relations

Despite their differences, almost throughout the 1990s, during the Afghan Civil War, Iran had expressed its support for Pakistan when Pakistan's Prime Minister Nawaz Sharif raised his concern with President Mohammad Khatami about India's nuclear tests. President Khatami said, "we regret what has happened and we are concerned about India's nuclear tests."[171]

He further added, "we regard Pakistan's security seriously and understand its position. The security of Pakistan, as a brother, friendly and neighbouring state, is crucial to us. We consider their issue to be extremely important and will stand by it."[172] Iran understood that India's nuclear tests in May 1998 had changed the geostrategic situation and the power balance. Despite divergence of their views on many issues, Iran greeted Pakistan's nuclear tests of May 28-30, 1998 as positive. Iran's Foreign Minister, Kamal Kharrazi was the first foreign dignitary to visit Islamabad on June 1, 1998[173] and congratulated Pakistan for its nuclear achievement by saying, "now, they (Muslims) feel confident, because a fellow Islamic nation possesses the knowhow to build nuclear weapons."[174] Iran's UN Envoy in Geneva, Ali Khorram, said, "India's blasts disrupted the strategic balance in the subcontinent...as a result of Pakistan following suite.[175] While Iran supported Pakistan's nuclear tests, India's May 11-13, 1998 nuclear tests became a source of concern for Iran.

9/11 Attacks, Iran's Nuke Problems, Iraq War, India factor and Iran-Pak Cooperation

The Iran's relation with Pakistan developed substantially with a host of new factors impinging the region in the early years of the twenty-first century. The first decade of the twenty-first century witnessed new changes not only on the regional sphere but also in the global sphere. The 9/11 attacks were reciprocated by the War on Terror by the US forces and Afghanistan became the ground. Soon Taliban forces were crushed by the US forces with a support base from Pakistan. Pakistan, which was among three other nations along with Saudi Arabia and UAE that had extended state recognition to Taliban government in 1998, broke with Taliban and readjusted its policies towards Afghanistan not only by supporting the US retaliation but also provided bases to the US Air Forces for such retaliation. This new development was a satisfactory one for the Iranian establishment.

The Taliban retreat from Kabul nudged Pakistan and Iran ending decade-old frosty relations and working to accommodate each other's strategic and economic interests in Afghanistan. After the Government of Pakistan broke with the Taliban, "serious difficulties that had marred relations between Islamabad and Tehran of late ceased to exist",[176] Iran's Foreign Minister, Kamal Kharazi, said during one of his visits to Islamabad in December 2001. The then Pakistani Foreign Minister, Abdul Sattar, also added, "The role of Pakistan with regard to the Taliban has been exaggerated as far as its influence with the militia was concerned." A former Foreign Minister, Sartaj Aziz, agreed that the ouster of the Taliban does remove a major irritant between Iran and Pakistan.[177] However, this new Pak-US realignment against Taliban witnessed a problem with Iranian policy makers who has been supporting the Northern Alliance in the yet-to-be reconstructed Afghanistan. This new development has coincided with Iran's nuke problems in the global scene.

In August 2002 the National Council for Resistance, an opposition group, exposed the nuclear sites at Natanz and Arak being developed by Iran.[178] This was followed by the Iraq War in March 2003 when the US made an attack against Iraq in the region changing Saddam Hussein's regime. Iran became concerned about the post-September 11, 2001 military cooperation between the US and Pakistan and the foreign power presence not only in Afghanistan but also in Iraq both of which shared common borders with Iran. Ironically, both Iran and Pakistan shared long-term perspectives on how to deal with the intrusiveness of foreign powers in the region. Both Iran and Pakistan, for instance, opposed the United States' unilateral action in Iraq, calling for a central role for the UN. During the last few years the Pakistani officials have repeatedly stated their steadfast opposition to any US military strike against Iran via Pakistani territory and/or airspace. Noticeably, Iran and Pakistan have taken several concrete steps, during last decade, to increase their security cooperation. Soon after the 9/11 attacks and US' retaliation against Afghanistan, in November 2001, the Pakistani-Iranian Joint Ministerial Commission on security was established primarily to deal with the problems of terrorism, smuggling, sectarian violence, extremism and narcotics. The initial meeting of this commission was held in September 2002. There has been a renewal in consultations between the foreign ministers of both countries on bilateral relations and on regional and international developments. Regular interactions between Pakistani and Iranian intelligence officials have been ongoing since October 2001. These interactions are held between senior-level Inter-Services Intelligence (ISI) and Iranian intelligence officials and focus on the future of Afghanistan, Iran's role in seven cultural centers in Pakistan etc. Both countries have agreed to solve security and border issues in a special security committee.

Iran-Pak Cooperation

During the first decade of the twenty-first century, there has been a new vigour in Iran-Pakistan relations, particularly because of the ouster of Taliban from power in Afghanistan. President Mohammad Khatami of Iran paid a state visit to Pakistan from December 23–25, 2002, his first ever and the first as an Iranian President in a decade (President Rafsanjani had visited Pakistan in 1992), was described as a turning point in Iran–Pakistan relationship.[179]

Incidentally, Iran was the first country that President Musharraf had paid a visit after he took over as the country's Chief Executive.[180] President Khatami was accompanied by a team of senior ministers and advisors. Their presence reflected the wide-ranging nature of discussions between the Iranian leader and Pakistan's new political leadership. President Khatami held official talks with President Musharraf and Prime Minister Mir Zafarullah Khan Jamali in two separate sessions on December 23 and 24. The talks covered the entire range of bilateral relations, as well as regional and international issues of mutual concerns. As a result of Khatami's visit, Iran and Pakistan signed four agreements and a memorandum of understanding (MoU) aimed at enhancing their bilateral relationship, mainly in the fields of trade, plant quarantine, science and technology. A four page joint communiqué issued at the conclusion of the two-day Khatami visit reflected the similarity of views on key strategic issues including Kashmir. It spoke of Islamabad and Tehran having "common strategic interests" and expressed the determination of the two sides to strengthen their bilateral relations in all spheres, including economic and defence.[181]

The Presidential visit was followed by an Iranian Economic delegation to attend the 13th session of joint Iran-Pak Economic Commission in January 2003. The Iranian delegation informed its Pakistani colleagues that 250 kilometres of the 550 kilometres stretch of Zahidan-Kerman railway section has been constructed and by 2005 the entire length will be constructed. Pakistani Prime Minister, Mir Zafarullah Khan Jamali paid a return visit in October 2003, which was described by some Pakistani circles as 'the most significant' and possibly 'the most fruitful' of all his foreign trips. The visit was undertaken to augment the multifaceted relations between the two countries, particularly in the economic sphere, as well as to promote greater identity of views on international and regional issues of mutual interest. An important outcome of this visit was that President Khatami expressed concern over Kashmir issue, and in the joint communiqué, Iran called for early and unconditional Indo-Pak talks to resolve the Kashmir dispute in accordance with the wishes of the Kashmiri people.[182] In March 2004, Iran's first vice president, Reza Aref, visited Pakistan. His talks centered on further strengthening the existing cooperation between the two countries.

In the summer of 2005, dramatic political changes took place in Iran. Rafsanjani suffered the serious electoral humiliation at the hands of

Ahmadinejad. While it marked a definite end to a 'corrupt establishment' as most Iranians believed, the electoral outcome of President Ahmadinejad had given rise to a bitter atmosphere in the country. In fact, the post-election atmosphere was so negative that Khamenei decided to refuse Ahmadinejad permission to publicly celebrate his victory.[183] This, in any case, not to deny, his undoubted, if partly engineered, electoral victory over Rafsanjani. President Ahmadinejad soon tried to dominate the domestic political landscape through a calibrated foreign policy. Resisting the foreign oppressor is so central to Iranian nationalist mythology, and so broad in its appeal that Ahmadinejad has been able to use it in his earlier capacity as Mayor and also currently in the capacity of President. Ironically such a policy has to be coterminous with a friendly policy towards friendly neighbours. This was observed in his policy towards Pakistan.

As soon as he was elected to the presidency of the Islamic Republic, in 2005, Ahmadinejad accelerated the bilateral relations between Iran and Pakistan. According to a report by the Media Department of Iranian Presidential Office, President Ahmadinejad, after receiving a written message of the then Pakistani President, Pervez Musharraf, from Mr. Rashid Ahmed, the then Pakistani Minister of Railways who was visiting Iran in May 2006, expressed hope that previously signed agreements between the two countries in different fields, including railways transportation, would be executed soon.[184] On May 16, 2006, Ahmadinejad said in Tehran: "Iran is for expansion of ties with Pakistan and Tehran will support cooperation with Islamabad in all fields."[185]

This was followed by a visit of the Pakistani foreign minister, Khurshid Ahmad Khan Kasuri, on December 20, 2006. Mr. Kasuri met the Iranian President, Mahmoud Ahmadinejad, and discussed the regional situation. In the meeting with Pak Foreign Minister at Kermanshah, Mr. Ahmadinejad said that strengthening friendly ties among Iran, Pakistan and Afghanistan would ensure regional peace and security.[186] He further added: "The regional countries have shared destinies and interests, which is a good reason for maintaining friendly attitude with one another." In the context of the nuclear controversy, Ahmadinejad said; "Pakistan's support for Iran's lawful rights in the International Atomic Energy Agency is a token of the existing grave friendly ties between the two countries." The President recalled his meeting with Musharraf on the sidelines of the UN summit in New York and said and said that he believed the Islamabad's positions have created a brilliant perspective for bilateral relations in future.

Musharraf stressed the need for strengthening ties between the two 'brotherly nations' and extended his invitation to Ahmadinejad to visit Pakistan. Describing the approach of his country towards Iran's nuclear issue as being "quite transparent," Musharraf said that both Pakistani government and nation were against use of force and exerting pressures against countries. Musharraf stressed that any solution to the problem should fall within framework of the International Atomic Energy Agency. He further noted that his country would do its best to have Iran's nuclear problem settled in the peaceful manner. [187]

Iran's voice was also echoed in Pakistan. The then Pakistani Prime Minister, Shaukat Aziz, in November 2007, said that Pakistan shares extensive ties with Iran "based upon faith, belief, joint history and culture. Expansion of cooperation in the fields of trade and investment can further strengthen the bilateral ties."[188] In recent years, Iran has equally reciprocated and President Ahmadinejad visited Pakistan in April 2008 to strengthen their bilateral ties. He expressed that "If Afghanistan goes out of control, Pakistan and Iran will feel the consequences. There is a very real danger of the war in Afghanistan spilling over mainly into Pakistan, but the consequences will also affect Iran".[189] Noticeably thereafter, in March 2009, President Asif Ali Zardari, Afghan President Hamid Karzai and Iranian President Mehmood Ahmadinejad had a trilateral meeting at Tehran. During the meeting, the leaders of the three neighbourly and "brotherly countries" discussed issues of mutual interest and concerns including the security situation in Afghanistan and in the region.[190] These political relationships, in the mean time, have also been converted to a broadening energy partnership.

In 2008, Iran and Pakistan met at the seventeenth session of their Joint Economic Commission, where Iranian foreign minister Manouchehr Mottaki claimed that Iran and Pakistan have the potential to increase their already-significant economic cooperation "far beyond the present volume of trade between them which is US $500 million annually." [191] At the meeting, the representatives of both the governments expressed their hope to increase their bilateral trade to $1 billion in the near future.[192] In June 2008, Iran and Pakistan cooperated in a number of trade groups and agreed on a list of 300 tradable items in an effort to stimulate mutual trade.[193] In August 2008, Iran agreed to finance a robust energy project that would allow Pakistan to import 1,000 megawatts of electricity to overcome its power shortage.[194]

The project, a $60 million endeavour, will run a 100-kilometer (62-mile) electric line to help augment the 40 megawatts of electricity Pakistan already receives daily from Iran. In February 2010, Punjab Chief Minister Muhammad Shahbaz Sharif called for the creation of an economic free-trade zone among Pakistan, Iran, Turkey and other Islamic countries. During a celebration of the Revolution Day of Iran, Sharif had noted that "deep, friendly relations exist between Pakistan and Iran and it is the need of the hour that socio-economic cooperation should be promoted." Iranian and Pakistani officials, in February 2010, signed the first memorandum of understanding (MoU) between the two countries on cross border trade. The MoU was penned during the two countries' first joint committee meeting on border trade in Iran's southeastern Sistan and Balochistan province. Iraj Hassanpour, the head of Sistan and Balochistan's trade organization, stated that "based on the MoU, the two countries are bound to hold public and specialized fairs at their common borders and in the capital of Sistan & Balochistan province, Zahedan, and Quetta in Pakistan." Both sides also decided to establish large storehouses to facilitate the storage of trade commodities at their border customs.

Sardar Muhammad Latif Khan Khosa, a Pakistani advisor to the prime minister on information technology, recently called for increased collaboration between Iran and Pakistan in telecommunications. During the last few years, Pakistan has taken every possible step to increase its bilateral relations with Iran. Pakistan's relations with Iran, in recent years, have been one of active engagement. During a July 30, 2009 interview with the Iranian Islamic Republic News Agency, Dr Ashfaq Hassan Khan, a former economic advisor in Pakistan, insisted that while economic ties between Iran and Pakistan should expand at all levels, cooperation in the energy sector is vital for Pakistan.[195] During a May 2010 conversation with Iran's ambassador to Pakistan, Mashallah Shakeri Khosa expressed his belief that increased bilateral activity in the sector has the potential to increase regional economic development and security. In May 2010, the two sides discussed building a part linking Iran and Pakistan of the Iran-Pakistan-India pipeline that would pump crude oil of Iran from the South Pars oil field to Pakistan. [196]

Iran-Pakistan-India Gas Pipeline

The Iran-Pakistan-India gas pipeline project reportedly was conceived as early as in 1989.[197] But in 1997 India, Iran and Pakistan agreed in principle to officially pursue the matter with urgency.[198] The proposed pipeline would run about 1,115 km in Iran, 705 km in Pakistan and 850 km in India, and total investment was estimated at $7 billion to complete.[199] The plan proposed by Iran envisaged a foreign consortium (Shell, British Gas, Petronas and an Iranian business group) that would buy gas from Iran and sell it to the stakeholders. At one stage, Iran even proposed that 30 per cent of the gas would be destined for Pakistan and 70 per cent for India, giving both countries a stake in maintaining the flow.[200]

Capital spending for the project was to be shared with Iran taking 48 per cent, with Pakistan taking 32 per cent, and with India 20 per cent. In India, the debate on the pipeline project was fairly polarised. Though there was consensus on the desirability of importing gas from Iran, opinions have been divided over the route. There could be four options to bring gas from Iran to India: first, via Pakistan land route, second, via shallow water of Pakistan, third, deep sea route and fourth, in the form of LNG. Apparently, the first option was the most cost effective, but given the Indo-Pak relations, its strategic feasibility was in question; the pipeline through 12 nautical miles into the territorial waters of Pakistan ruled out Indian participation, while deep water in the sea would be cost prohibitive.[201] GAIL (India) and NIOC engaged a UK company Gardline Surveys to conduct marine survey of offshore pipeline at the cost of $4.3 million, but the company failed to finish the assignment because, as it informed to Indo-Iranian Joint Committee, the "critical equipment for the survey was not available due to US sanctions on Iran".[202] The Ministry of External Affairs of India has been persistent that 'any thaw with Islamabad will not include oil'.[203] Amidst such a consistent Indian position till recently, Pakistan had been pleading for signing a deal with Iran on a bilateral platform.

Iran-Pakistan Gas Deal and signing the Agreement

Pakistan, although was eager to sign an agreement with Iran on a bilateral forum, had repeatedly been dissuaded from going ahead with negotiations on the Iran-Pakistan-India (IPI) pipeline. American displeasure had been made apparent to Pakistan on a number of occasions within the last couple of years. The then US Energy Secretary, Samuel Bodman, while visiting Pakistan in March 2005, publicly expressed Washington's disapproval at the gas pipeline project.[204] In a meeting with Pakistani Foreign Minister, Khurshid Mehmood Kasuri, in Washington, in June 2005, the US Secretary of State, Condoleeza Rice, also reiterated Washington's position that the proposed pipeline was against US laws.[205] Rice argued that even if the US administration gave up its opposition to the pipeline, there were powerful lobbies in Congress, the media, and academia that would continue to oppose the project and it would negatively impact the ties between the United States and Pakistan. But Kasuri emphasized the economic and political benefits of the proposed pipeline and said that it would allow Pakistan not only to earn up to $600 million a year from the pipeline, but also to import about $1 billion worth of gas every year from Iran.

Contrary to US pressure, recently, on 12 June 2010, both Iran and Pakistan, finalized a multi-billion dollar deal. Both the Iranian and Pakistani governments voiced their optimism that the gas would begin traversing the pipeline by 2014. This $7.5-billion project would allow Iran to supply Pakistan with up to 750 million cubic feet of gas daily, starting in 2014.[206] Iran planned to extend a pipeline from its giant South Pars gas field, through the city of Iranshahr in the southeast and on to its Chabahar port on the Persian Gulf, to the border with Pakistan (a total distance of around 750 miles). From there the a 440-mile Pakistani portion of the pipeline aimed to link the border with Nawabshah in Sindh province, north of Karachi.[207] Iran has already constructed 907 kilometres of the pipeline between the Asalooyeh Energy Zone and Iranshahr. The cost for the Pakistan section of the project is estimated at $1.65 billion. The "sovereign guarantee" agreement was signed by S.R. Kasaezadeh, Managing Director of the National Iranian Oil Company, and Irshad Kaleemi, Joint Secretary of Pakistan's Ministry of Petroleum and Natural Resources. Pakistani Petroleum Minister Naveed Qamar and Secretary Kamran Lashari attended the signing ceremony.[208] Under the gas sale and purchase agreement (GSPA), Pakistan will import 750 million cubic feet a day (mmcfd) with a provision to increase it to one billion cubic feet a day (bcfd). The volume of imported gas will be about 20 per cent of Pakistan's current gas production and the agreement is for a period of 25 years, renewable for another five years. The gas will be provided to the power sector to generate about 5,000 megawatts of electricity. As a part of the conditions precedent (CPs) to be completed by the parties to make the agreement effective, the government of Pakistan is providing a "performance guarantee" on behalf of the Inter State Gas Company. The Pakistani petroleum minister said that construction of the pipeline would create jobs, provide vocational training and develop backward areas of Pakistani provinces of Balochistan and Sindh. "The IP project will be another testimony of the long historic and cordial relations between Pakistan and Iran," Mr. Qamar said.[209]

The Iran-Pakistan agreement represented a breach in US efforts to isolate Iran economically, and reflected Pakistan's desperate need for energy and its reluctance to subordinate its economic security needs to US pressure. The Pakistani Foreign Ministry spokesman, Abdul Basit, also stressed that the sanctions resolution passed by the Security Council were not applicable in any way to what he called "purely a commercial agreement."[210] Although U.S. officials in both the Bush and Obama administrations, have not said directly whether the Iran-Pakistan pipeline would be sanctioned under the Iran Sanctions Act (ISA), State Department spokesman Philip Crowley had warned of "ramifications" for those doing business with Iran. Responding to a question about the pipeline plans earlier, he said that part of U.S. dialogue with India and Pakistan was "to understand and help with the respective and legitimate energy needs that countries in the region have."[211] "But we are also sending a very strong signal ... to those countries that have economic relations with Iran or to those sectors of the global economy that do business with Iran." However, no such sanctions have taken place as yet. It may be added that the Iran – Libya Sanctions Act (ILSA), which was in place since 1996 with continuous renewal and currently excludes Libya, requires that sanctions be imposed on foreign companies that make an 'investment' of more than $20 million per year in Iran's energy sector. Although Iran's oil and gas sector was not directly targeted by the resolution, legislation currently before Congress aimed at imposing unilateral U.S. sanctions against Tehran to punish companies that help Iran's energy industry, including building or maintaining oil or gas pipelines, or sell petroleum products to Iran. The ISA definition of "investment," according to an April 2010 Congressional Research Service report, "is interpreted by the State Department to include pipelines to or through Iran, as well as upgrades or expansions of such energy related projects as refineries." But Pakistan has been trying to convince the United States that it will not be violating any US law by agreeing to build the gas pipeline. Ironically, the Pakistani Ambassador to Tehran, Mohammad Bakhsh Abbasi, recently pleaded that sanctions targeting the Iranian energy sector will have no affect on the construction of the multi-billion-dollar Iran-Pakistan gas pipeline project. The Iranians have reacted vehemently to the US pressure. Iran's Oil Minister, Bijan Namdar Zangeneh, went on record to say, 'It is unreasonable to prevent Pakistan from accessing Iranian gas. Energy markets should be depoliticized. We sell crude oil and LNG. Why can't we be allowed to sell piped gas? Accordingly the Iranian part of the project will be financed entirely by Iran and a group of multinational investors, which Iran will put together. Pakistan's investment is to begin only after the pipeline reaches Pakistan's territory. Interestingly Beijing has expressed its readiness that it would be willing to extend the project if India opts out of the project. China has been looking at Pakistan to access the hydrocarbon rich states of West Asia to follow on its success in building oil and gas pipelines from Myanmar. Chinese firms are looking forward to cash on the IP pipeline project and are looking at broadening their involvement. Hence Iran-Pakistan relations are not limited to a bilateral relationship alone. Rather they are marching towards a triangular relationship with the involvement of China as well in the vital energy sector.

Mutual Frictions and Concerns

Iran, in recent years, although benefited immensely from Pakistan's nuclear programme, has been more concerned, among other things, about the secrecy of a Saudi-Pakistani agreement in nuclear matters. There was a high-level visit to Pakistan by a Saudi prince in 2003 after a Saudi defense official's visit to Pakistan's nuclear facilities, prompting to such speculations in Tehran. Although Saudi officials have denied rumors of an oil-for-nukes pact between Riyadh and Islamabad, the Iranian policymakers are put on guard by such rumors, deemed credible in the light of Pakistan's history, its close ties to Saudi Arabia, and its cash dependency on the oil-rich Saudis.

In Islamabad, there are questions regarding Tehran's military support to Afghan leaders of Northern Alliance. Further Iran's friendly overtures in providing India a better position in Afghanistan is also viewed with concern by Pakistani government. A section of the Pakistani establishment has also been critical of Iran's decision to upgrade the Chabahar port facilities to make the Mumbai–Chabahar route functional for trade between India and the Central Asian republics. However, Pakistan's attitude has always been tinged with India colour and Pakistan remain apprehensive of India's increased presence in Iran, and the strategic implications of the Indian Consulate set up at Bandar Abbas in May 2002 (after the closure of its Consulate in Shiraz). Pakistan complains that the Consulate, through monitoring devices, will be able to follow movement of ships throughout the Persian Gulf, especially through the Strait of Hormuz. These apprehensions of Pakistan have been present since then. Similarly Iran has been complaining about the terrorist activities conducted by Jundallah group which is promoted by the Pakistani establishment in recent years.

Jundallah Terrorism and Iran-Pakistan Relations

Jundallah, a Pakistan-based Sunni terrorist outfit, has been carrying out terrorist activities on Iranian territories that have an abiding impact on emerging Iran-Pakistan relations and consequently the politics of the region. Jundallah hit the headlines in October 2009 when, at least, 42 people were killed because of two major attacks it launched on the Iranian province of Sistan-Balochistan. Among them were four of the most senior commanders of the Islamic Revolution Guards Corps (IRGC), Iran's elite military unit. They included Generals Noor Ali Shooshtari (the deputy commander of IRGC land forces), Rajab Ali Mohammad-Zadeh (the commander of IRGC forces in the Sistan and Balochistan province), Hossein Moradi (commander of the IRGC garrison in the county of Iranshahr) and Ali Alavian (the commander of the IRGC's "Sarallah" Corps — a prestigious infantry unit). This is the biggest blow against the IRGC since the days of the Iran-Iraq war in the 1980s.[212] The attacks were widely condemned by the UN as well as by the US, the UK and Pakistan.[213]

Within Iran, there was severe condemnation on the attacks at all levels. Ayatollah Seyyed Ali Khamenei, Iran's Supreme Leader, in his speech to the nation, emphasised: "The crime committed by the blood thirsty Jundallah revealed the satanic face of the enemies of security and unity, who are backed by some espionage services and oppressor governments."[214] Mahmoud Ahmadinejad, the Iranian President, was more direct in his accusation of Pakistan when he said, "We were informed that some security agents in Pakistan are cooperating with the main elements of this terrorist incident".[215] Iranian Foreign Minister, Manouchehr Mottaki, charged the Jundallah with launching regular attacks inside the Islamic Republic after illegally crossing the Iran-Pakistan border.[216] In a strong warning, he stated that Iran would not only seal the border with Pakistan near Balouchistan but also attack specific hideouts of Jundallah inside Pakistan. He also spoke of sending an investigative team to Pakistan to look into the matter. Subsequently Mustafa Mohammad Najjar, the Interior Minister, met his Pakistani counterpart, Rehman Malik, at Islamabad. Mr. Najjar had brought out the fact that Iran had sufficient evidence to prove the involvement of Abdol Malek Rigi, the Chief of Jundallah, in the attacks. He also alleged that Rigi was known to conduct his terror campaigns from various hideouts In Pakistan and hence stated that he should be handed over to Iran.

Jundallah ('Soldiers of Allah' in Arabic) which claims to be fighting for the rights of Sunni Muslims in Iran was founded in 2002 and was later renamed as the People's Resistance Movement of Iran.[217] In December 2006, the group kidnapped seven Iranian soldiers from the city of Zahedan, in south-eastern Iran. In February 2007, the group killed 11 members of the IRGC in a car bombing near Zahedan. In December 2008, it carried out a suicide car attack on the headquarters of a joint police and narcotics unit in the town of Saravan, Iran, killing four officers besides injuring many others. It claimed the responsibility for the suicide attack inside the Ameer al-Momenin mosque in Zahedan, Iran, in May 2009 that killed 25 people and wounded at least 125 others. Jundallah claims to have killed more than 400 Iranian nationals during the last six years.

Jundallah is presently led by Abdol Malek Rigi and is believed to have more than 1,000 fighters. During an interrogation at a Quetta jail, Abdul Hamid Rigi, the brother Abdol Malek Rigi, maintained that the group was formed to protect the rights of the Irani Balouch people who are mainly Sunni. The group is reported to have developed strong links with the Taliban, the Inter-Services Intelligence (ISI) of Pakistan, Lashkar-e-Jhangvi (an anti-Shiite group based in Punjab), as well as the Al-Qaeda for enlarging its area of operation and support system.[218] Because of its Sunni sectarianism, the group is believed to be receiving regular support from these organisations and has developed well planned terror tactics targeted to influence Iran's theocratic Shiia politics.

Tehran has consistently criticised the Pakistani Government for its support to Jundallah and had lodged a severe protest with Islamabad after the Momenin Mosque attack. Reportedly, the Iranian authorities had told the Pakistani ambassador in Iran that the three terrorists involved in the incident, Haji Noti Zehi, Gholam Rasoul Shahi Zehi and Zabihollah Naroui, should be publicly hanged. Iran also alleged that the Zahedan suicide attack could have been averted had Islamabad acted in time on the Iranian intelligence inputs provided to them. Earlier, on March 20, 2009 the Iranian ambassador to Pakistan, Mashallah Shakeri, after the disappearance of an Iranian diplomat from Peshawar in 2008, had addressed an unusual press conference in Islamabad and blamed Jundallah for the act. He also accused Pakistan of allowing its soil being used by Jundallah terrorists against Iran. Shakeri had asked Islamabad specifically to curb its anti-Iran activities by taking a decisive action against the group's leadership. He also indicated that Iran would inflict heavy punishment on Jundullah members if captured. In fact, Iran had already resorted to increasingly tough measures against the group. An example of this was, in July 2009, 13 of Jundallah members were hung in a mass prison execution, after being found as "Enemies of God".

The Pakistani Foreign Office, as always, has denied providing any support to Jundallah.[219] But Abdol Hamid Rigi, who is on a death row after being captured and convicted by Iranian authorities, has candidly accepted that their main support comes from the Pakistani Government. In a press conference held at Tehran he stated that Jundullah operates primarily for two reasons. The first was because he claimed that an overwhelming number of Balochis in Iran, who are Sunni, suffer discrimination from the Shiia regime there. The second, despite living along strategic trade routes atop a wealth of untapped hydrocarbon and mineral deposits, this Balochi minority has not come out from deep poverty and repression because of the step motherly treatment given to them by the Shia Government. No doubt, Jundallah is a sectarian organisation with a support base from Pakistan. The group is already designated as a terrorist organisation and banned in Iran. But neither the Pakistan Government nor the US Administration, has made any such effort for a ban. However, Jundalah's activities in recent years has not only created acrimony in Iran-Pakistan relations but also has sent shock waves in the region.

Renewed Mutual Assistance:

(a) Iran's Nuke Issue and Support from Pakistan:

It must be highlighted here that Pakistan's policy towards Iran has been very friendly, despite some minor sectarian clashes. It has already been reflected in the recent IAEA meetings in November 2009 when it abstained against the voting of Iran.[220] It must be added that, in the mean time, in May 2009.the Iranian President Mahmoud Ahmadinejad hosted a meeting with Afghan President Hamid Karzai and Pakistani President Asif Ali Zardari for talks which focussed on rebuilding war-torn Afghanistan.[221] Recently on 11 January 2010, in a meeting with his Pakistani counterpart, Asif Ali Zardari, the Iranian President, Mahmoud Ahmadinejad had warned against the enemies' [USA, Israel, UK] conspiracies to destabilize the [Asian] region, and urged cooperation among all 57 OIC member states. Zardari further said that strong Iran and Pakistan are in the interest of security and stability in the region.[222]

Iran-Pak Organisational and Communicational Links

Apart from the pure bilateral activities, both Iran and Pakistan are also active in multilateral forums where they can develop mutual relations. One such forum is the Economic Cooperation Organization (ECO), a trade and investment group. The ECO is an intergovernmental regional organization established in 1985 by Iran, Pakistan and Turkey for the purpose of promoting economic, technical and cultural cooperation among the Member States.[223] It is the successor organization of Regional Cooperation for Development (RCD) which remained in existence since 1964 up to 1979. In 1992, the Organization was expanded to include seven new members, namely: Islamic Republic of Afghanistan, Republic of Azerbaijan, Republic of Kazakhstan, Kyrgyz Republic, Republic of Tajikistan, Turkmenistan and Republic of Uzbekistan.[224] It is said that Pakistan perceived the territorial configurations of the ECO and a web of strategic interests around it as a way to contain India's potential influence in the region. Since Iran and Pakistan also hold observer status in the Shanghai Cooperation Organization (SCO) (an Asian regional security group),[225] their membership has provided them another opportunity for interaction in their areas of mutual interests. Ironically Pakistan has helped encourage trilateral trade with Iran (and Turkey) in commercial goods, as well as infrastructure development beyond the programs as administered by the ECO.

Currently Iran and Pakistan are planning to establish a railway from Gwadar (an emerging Pakistani port at Arabian Sea) to Taftan in Iran via Saindak, a resource rich region of Pakistan's Baluchistan province. Saindak and Taftan have already been linked via a 33- kilometer railway.[226] The Saindak project was abandoned in 1995 but was revived in 2010 with Chinese financial assistance of $30 million for copper and gold production.[227] If a railway from Quetta (the provincial capital of Baluchistan) to Taftan (in Iran) is developed, it will not only accelerate trade between Iran and Pakistan but also will help Pakistan to develop its trade links with many Central Asian countries. A road from Gwadar to Saindak running parallel to Iran-Pakistan border will make it the shortest route to reach Central Asia from the Arabian Sea. Further, Pakistan is also hoping to cash on its deep friendship by a $60 billion transit fees over 20 years from Persian oil shipments that will be meant for China from Iran through the Gwadar port.[228] It is argued that this step of Pakistan will strengthen not only its bilateral relations with Iran but also its triangular relationship with China.

It is argued that China also has a strategic desire not only to reduce its dependency on the sea lanes which are traditionally being patrolled by the US navy but also open an overland shipment of oil and gas, for which the Pakistani port, Gwadar is a key point.[229]

It may be noted that Pakistan has sincerely attempted to develop its trade links through meaningful dialogues not only in bilateral levels but also in regional levels. Pakistan's attempt to bring a "friendly Iran" to its side has also been reflected in various high level visits from Iran to Pakistan. Recently, the leaders of Pakistan welcomed the visit of President Ahmadinejad to flood-hit areas of Pakistan and said: "it would help in further strengthening the two countries' brotherly ties". Senator Haji Muhammad Adeel of Awami National Party expressing his views said: "Iran is our brotherly Islamic neighbour and has always helped Pakistan in hard times". "Iran is our brother and has always supported Pakistan in times of pain," he added. "We also appreciate the aid that our brotherly neighbour (Iran) has sent for flood victims," said Pervez Rashid. Tariq Azeem Khan, Senator of Pakistan Muslim League-Q. He also said: "We have a special relationship with Iran," he added.[230] Hence, a Pakistan-Iran relation, on the whole, during the period, has been a friendly one and poised to develop further in near future.

(b) Kashmir Crisis and Iran's Support to Pakistan

Iran, both in the past and in recent years, not only in bilateral forums but also in multilateral organisations, had supported Pakistan on Kashmir issue. Imam Khomeini had once declared:

> *"Today it is the duty of the heads of Islamic countries, the kings and the presidents of Islamic countries to put aside these petty differences which occasionally arise between them. There are no Arabs and non-Arabs, Turks and Persians; there is only Islam and unity under Islam. They should adopt the same method of struggle that the Prophet of Islam used in his struggle; they should follow the way of Islam. If they guard their ideological unity, if they put aside these petty differences, if all the Muslims join together, then, according to estimations, there will be a community of seven hundred million. But seven hundred million people divided are not as great as one million united. Seven hundred million divided people are of no use, thousands of millions of divided people cannot do anything either. However, if these seven hundred million, if only four hundred million of them, two hundred*

million of them, were to unite together, join hands in brotherhood together, protect each other's borders, protect their own boundaries, if they were to unite in the Islamic community which is common to us all, in the religion of monotheism which is common to us all, in the Islamic interests that we share, then the Jews would no longer covet Palestine and India would no longer have designs on Kashmir."[231]

Iran had extended support to Pakistan on Kashmir issue both in bilateral and multilateral forums. In the historic Casablanca Conference, in a declaration in December 1994, Iran had called for the resolution of the Kashmir dispute in accordance with United Nations Resolutions.[232] During the visit of President Rafsanjani to Pakistan in 1995, he had also exchanged views and concluded that the oppression to which the people of Kashmir were subjected remained a source of tension not only for Pakistan but also for the region. President Rafsanjani had declared in the Parliament of Pakistan that "Kashmir issue is your problem and it is also our problem too, because it is an Islamic problem".[233] President Rafsanjani had underlined the importance of finding a solution to the Kashmir problem in accordance with the relevant United Nations resolutions and through meaningful negotiation.[234] President Khatami, during his visit to Pakistan, in December 2002, had referred, on Kashmir, to the need for negotiations and for a solution keeping in view the will of the Kashmiri people. Maintaining that he was speaking as a Muslim and as an Iranian, he expressed deep anguish at the brutalities and sufferings inflicted on the Kashmiri people and asked that these should come to an end.[235] Recently, Iran's Supreme Leader, Ayatollah Ali Khamenei, appealed to the Muslim elite worldwide to back the "struggle" in Jammu and Kashmir, equating the northern Indian state with that of Afghanistan, Iraq and Pakistan. He said:

"Today the major duties of the elite of the Islamic Ummah is to provide help to the Palestinian nation and the besieged people of Gaza, to sympathize and provide assistance to the nations of Afghanistan, Pakistan, Iraq and Kashmir, to engage in struggle and resistance against the aggressions of the United States and the Zionist regime," Khamenei said in a message to Haj pilgrims. IRNA news agency quoted him as saying that Muslims should be united and "spread awakening and a sense of responsibility and commitment among Muslim youth throughout Islamic communities".[236]

OIC, Iran and Jammu and Kashmir

The Organization of Islamic Conference (OIC) was established upon a decision of the historical summit which took place in Rabat, Kingdom of Morocco on 12th Rajab 1389 Hijra (25 September 1969) as a result of criminal arson of Al-Aqsa Mosque in occupied Jerusalem.[237] It established specific groups and branches thereafter which operate to fulfil OIC charter. For example, the OIC Mission in Vienna (UNOV) was established in 1980 and also in Geneva in 1992 which were accredited to the United Nations Office in Vienna and Geneva respectively. [238] In 1999, the Parliamentary Union of the OIC member states (PUOICM) was established in Iran in 1999 and its head office is situated in Tehran.[239] The OIC has been very active and takes important decisions that can influence the UN on various important disputes, not necessarily international in character. Iran is an important and influential member of the OIC but surprisingly, detriment to India's interests, on several occasions, has expressed serious concerns over the bilateral dispute of Jammu and Kashmir between India and Pakistan. In March 1994, Islamabad had succeeded in securing the passage of a resolution in OIC condemning reported violations of human rights by the Indian troops in Kashmir at the summit meeting of the Organization of the Islamic Conference (OIC) held in Casablanca, Morocco.[240] In spite of a serious effort by the then Indian Prime Minister, P V Narasimha Rao, who had sent an ailing Defence Minister, Mr. Dinesh Singh, to Tehran urging Iran's indulgence in India's favour (since the OIC, like the IAEA, too had a convention that all decisions had to be arrived at through consensus) the OIC voted unanimously to pass the resolution against India for the "so-called human rights violation" in Jammu and Kashmir. In April 1994, when the UNHRC was assembling in Geneva, India faced an ugly situation. Technically, if the UNHRC in Geneva adopted a resolution condemning India for grave human rights violations in Jammu and Kashmir, a pathway would have opened for any of India's detractors (not only Pakistan) for referral of the 'Kashmir problem' to the UN in New York (The crisis was comparable to what could happen recently if the IAEA indeed decided on a UN Security Council referral apropos of the Iran's 'nuclear problem').[241] However, India managed to kill the OIC resolution in the UN.

Similarly, in the Doha Conference of OIC, in November 2000, Iran supported the resolution that demanded the UN for a plebiscite in Kashmir.[242] During the Amarnath land transfer imbroglio in 2008, Iran supported the OIC's condemnation of the "excessive and unwarranted use of force against the Kashmiri people".[243] The Secretary-General Ekmeleddin Ihsanoglu, on the sidelines of the 11th OIC Summit held at Dakar, Senegal in March 2008, described Kashmir as one of the oldest unresolved issues on the agenda of the UN and OIC. He also called upon the member states, especially those who have good relations with India (meaning Iran), to effectively use their influence to improve the human rights conditions in Kashmir.[244] But it was met by an Indian response that said: "The OIC has once again chosen to comment upon Jammu and Kashmir and India's internal affairs on which it has no *locus standi*."[245]

Recently, on 30 January 2010, the Iranian Majlis Speaker, Ali Larijani, called for a stronger role in OIC. He emphasised for establishing contacts with Muslims living in non-Islamic countries. "Contact with Muslim minorities living in non-Islamic states and making efforts to restore their rights" are among issues that the OIC parliamentary union must adopt through a logical, orderly and efficient procedure, Larijani told the sixth summit of Parliamentary Union of the Organization of the Islamic Conference in Kampala, Uganda. Larijani said a considerable number of Muslims have succeeded to find seats in parliaments in non-Muslim states and this can greatly help to defend the rights of Muslim minorities.[246]

In recent years the OIC, on the bilateral dispute between India and Pakistan on Kashmir, has become very critical of India's actions in Jammu and Kashmir. It has not only constituted a Contact Group on Kashmir but also accorded an observer status to the All Parties Hurriyat Conference (APHC) in OIC. It has also appointed a special envoy for Jammu and Kashmir. The perusal of the proceedings of this organization for the past two decades, more particularly after the APHC was accorded an observers status, are full of statements and resolutions in support of the right to self-determination for the people of Jammu and Kashmir.[247] India never permitted the OIC special envoy to visit Kashmir. The envoy has been visiting the "Azad Kashmir" and submitting its report to the organization. However, the OIC Contact Group as well as the general body has been passing resolutions in support of resolving the Kashmir problem. The ministerial meeting of the Organization of the Islamic Conference (OIC) Contact Group on Jammu and Kashmir that included Pakistan, Iran, Niger, Saudi Arabia and Turkey as well as the annual coordination committee of the OIC foreign ministers also took place during the 65th annual session of UN General Assembly at New York from 22 September to 24 September 2010.[248] The meeting was held at a time when Kashmir was once again burning. Ironically, the Iranian Foreign Ministry spokesman, Ramin Mehmanparast, expressed deep concern over the recent "crackdown in Indian-administered Kashmir". On 13 September 2010, Ramin Mehmanparast spoke out against the Indian government and five days later went to the extent of saying that to counter such protests could be "interpreted as supporting acts of sacrilege." He said it was "perfectly acceptable for Muslims to react to the desecration of the Koran" and called upon the Indian government to show "self-restraint".[249] The constant outrage from Tehran upset New Delhi, which finally decided to call in the Iranian envoy to the Ministry of External Affairs and deliver a strong protest. The same was conveyed simultaneously by the Indian mission in Tehran to Iranian authorities.[250] India, sources said, made it clear that maintaining law and order in Jammu and Kashmir was India's internal matter and Iran had no right to interfere or comment on these issues.[251] More so because the Press TV allegedly showed clips that were "unverified". The comments made by Iran and the subsequent protests were against the healthy momentum building up in the relationship during the past few months. So it has been observed that Iran has supported Pakistan not only in bilateral forums but also in multilateral organisations.

Iran's relation with Pakistan, during the past two decades, has witnessed fluctuations. These fluctuations have been mainly because of a host of factors. These fluctuations, on the negative side, have been mainly influenced by the factors relating to Afghanistan and Jundullah terrorism at the regional level, on a positive side, they have been influenced by Pakistan's political support to Iran on nuclear issues and Iran's support to Pakistan not only on energy issues but also on anti-India bashing. It has been a phase which has witnessed acknowledged complementarity between the two that has provided them wider scope for mutual benefit and cooperation.

5

CONCLUSION

Iran's relation with Pakistan, over the years, has been shaped by both constant and changing variables: They can be summarised mainly as domestic factors, ethnic Afghanistan and regional Gulf factors, India factor and the Super Power factor. Although for Pakistan it has been mainly the India factor that has taken a lead role in her foreign policy approach towards Iran, for Iran it has been a combination of a host of factors where her national interests were accorded top priority. Iran's relation with Pakistan and vice versa can be viewed from this angle.

During 1947-79, while the Shah was trying to build a country without relinquishing any portion of Iran's territory to any other nation, he was very much concerned in keeping the Communist threat from the Soviet Union at a disposable distance. Shah's support to Pakistan against India, during both the wars, was reflected as a combined result of both Iran and Pakistan's tilt towards the USA, their fear of Communism and Soviet Union and also India's friendly attitude towards the Soviet Union. Afghanistan, no doubt, has been a complex buffer spot for Iran and Pakistan in shaping their bilateral relations.

If Shah's regime is divided into various phases, it can be observed that, during the early 1950s till 1960s, the Shah had pursued a security policy that gave him a dominant position both in the immediate vicinity and the Persian Gulf. During the 1970s, Iran pursued a policy of strategy that had its security perimeter even beyond the Gulf. Ironically Iran's relation with Pakistan had become one of the corner stones for such a security policy. It may be mentioned that, in the post-1971 period, when the Shah was busy in projecting Iran's role beyond the Gulf, in the Strait of Hormuz, Gulf of Oman and the Arabian Sea as far as Babel-Mandeb, Pakistan was taken into confidence as a major pillar in supporting Iran's policy of security and strategy. Iran eventually planned to control the sea-lanes of the Indian Ocean. The Shah justified Iran's new and enlarged security perimeter by arguing that its sea-lanes in those areas were threatened indirectly by guerrilla attacks, through political subversion on land and also by conventional naval forces of anti-Iranian states. The Iranian policy towards Pakistan, during this period, was governed by a scenario called the "threat of encirclement" where Pakistan was perceived not only as a major bulwark but also a major supporter for the Shah. This is understandable in the context of India, Afghanistan, Baluchistan, Communism and Cold War rivalry.

The Bangladesh Crisis, the Indo-Soviet treaty, the Indo-Pakistani war of December 1971 and the threat perception of further dismemberment of Pakistan were all treated as potential dangers to Iran. The Shah not only treated them as dangers to Iranian security, he took further steps to secure both his land as well as sea frontiers. Hence not only Pakistan got a special importance in Iran's security policy, the Shah took appropriate measures in increasing Iranian naval capability in India's vicinity. The construction of bases on the Gulf of Oman, Arabian Sea and Indian Ocean complex which were decided in 1972, were all important steps that suggest Iran's desire to be counted as an Indian Ocean power. The contingency of a naval threat from India too was not altogether ruled out. India was growing into a major regional naval power. It operated well-balanced through somewhat outmoded weapon systems. A large part of its operational vessels like the submarines, the Osa missile boats and the frigates were of Soviet origin. It had effectively blockaded Pakistan during the 1971 war, not only in the Bay of Bengal but also in the Arabian Sea that washes the Iranian coast also. Pakistan was not a weak power by any means and hence India's war-time exploits did raise several security questions in Iran. This was true not only during the "encirclement" era (1971-74) but also in the long-term strategic balance thereafter.

The Soviet naval presence in the Indian Ocean, especially in the Arabian Sea region that astride the oil lanes, was also projected a threat to Iran's security. It was argued that Soviet political and even military presence in Iraq, especially at Umm al-Qasr, especially after the Soviet-Iraqi treaty of 1972, constituted a naval threat to Iran, The Shah, in an Interview in June 1972, when asked about Soviet bases in Iraq, said that one could not prevent military vessels of another country from paying visits anywhere in international waters. But if there should be a question of bases, it is obvious that it would create an entirely new situation. Despite the fact that the Iraqis had denied that they had offered base facilities to the Soviets, the western scholars and statesmen persisted in projecting that scenario to justify Iran's Gulf policy. Some scholars did not stop at an indirect threat from the USSR but projected direct Soviet submarine threat to western and Iranian shipping in the area, especially outside the Gulf.

During 1979-1989, unstable state situation and regime legitimacy in both Iran and Pakistan combined with a favourable state situation in Afghanistan with the withdrawal of Soviet Union were important events which were instrumental in bringing both Iran and Pakistan closer. The regional Gulf situation has also been a factor in such a friendly tie between the two. It was observed that during the Iran-Iraq War, despite pressures from Saudi Arab, Pakistan peculiarly supported Iran against Iraq- a Sunni dominated state in the region. It can be said that Iran was an important country in the region and was also seeking a more influential and dominating status in the Persian Gulf after the Iranian revolution and Pakistan was busy in creating an anti-India Islamic role that shaped their friendship during this period. Pakistan had to moderate its policies of anti-Shia measures and atrocities because of a threat perception of Shiism after the export of the Iranian Revolution since that had sent shock waves to all the Sunni regimes in power. In fact, Pakistan's support to Iran's nuclear programme and the religious support provided to General Zia by the Government of Imam Khomeini, can be construed as a policy that served the mutual interest of Reza Shah Pahlavi and General Zia ul-Haq during this period. The period was a friendly one in both Iran-Pakistan relationship.

During the early 1990s, Iran had a smooth relationship with Pakistan. But the Afghanistan situation played a crucial role which destroyed some of the merits of a burgeoning relationship between the two. The collapse of Soviet Union in 1990-91 and the rise and growth of hostile Taliban regime in neighbouring Afghanistan were considered as dual threats to Iran's relation with Pakistan. They remained so until the advent of the 9/11 attacks of 2001 when the situation could be exploited favourably both by Iran and Pakistan. Both Iran and Pakistan mitigated most of their frictions thereafter. In recent years it has gone to a very favourable position because of strategic efforts from both sides. Pakistan's political support to Iran during its international isolation in nuclear field and signing the Iran-Pakistan Gas Pipe Line deal against US pressure are a few examples among those strategic efforts.

Hence, It is quite arguable that Iran's relations with Pakistan, whether pursued under a monarchy (1947-78) or under a hard-line Islamic regime (1979-89) or a theocracy of moderate and hard-line mix of ruling elites (1990-2010), have been mainly guided by her national interests and priorities. Although for Pakistan it has been mainly the India factor that has taken a lead role in her foreign policy approach towards Iran, for Iran it has been a combination of a host of factors. Iran's relation with Pakistan can be substantiated from this angle. Iran has discovered in Pakistan, during her necessity, a new role for her national security building scheme and Pakistan has also capitalised on this relationship. Although these relations have been pursued within a bilateral framework, nonetheless, they have created sufficient scope for mutual relations within a multilateral framework. The nature of such a relationship, if accelerated, can have a number of implications, both short term and long term, both for the region and the globe.

First, the nature of the regional issue of Afghanistan will have its wider impact since both Iran and Pakistan are two major and active neighbours of Afghanistan. Though both Iran and Pakistan have extended their traditional support for different power groups such as the Northern Alliance and Taliban respectively in reshaping Afghanistan, their close relationship might also prompt them to support one of the above groups. In that case, it will create problems not only for regional powers like India but also for extra regional powers like the US. Since India's policy, in recent years, have both tilted towards the US and been critical of Iran's policy, India will face a catch twenty-two situation. Neither Taliban nor an Iran-dominated Northern Alliance will serve India's interests in Afghanistan, to speak less about India's policies in Central Asia, where Iran is also an important player.

Further the relationship between a nuclear armed Pakistan and an Islamic Iran will pose a grave danger not only to US forces in the region but also to powers which are friendly to US. The danger posed by an "Islamic bomb" from Iran with a support from Muslim Pakistan will no doubt spell deeper problems for India, an important regional player, that has a substantial chunk of Muslim minority and problems in Jammu and Kashmir but also will spell deeper threats to the regional security (with imminent threats for Israel). India will be affected because of Pakistan's policy of "India-bashing" that is limited not to Jammu and Kashmir only but spans elsewhere in the Indian subcontinent. The bilateral relationship can also pose a serious threat to India's' energy security policies pursued both in the Persian Gulf and Central Asia. Precisely for this, India cannot afford to shoulder an Iran-US hostility at the moment. A bilateral relationship between Iran and Pakistan, if converted further to a trilateral axis[252], as has been highlighted by scholars, with the inclusion of China through various friendly engagements, then India will face serious challenges in its immediate neighbourhood with sinister effects on its West Asian, Asian and global power- making and outlook.

As the focus of India's interest in West Asia is and would remain on the desirability of having (a) friendly governments (b) regional peace and stability (c) access to oil and gas resources (d) freedom of navigation in the Persian Gulf and through the Straits of Hormuz (e) continued market access for Indian trade, technology, investments and workforce and (f) security and welfare of the Indian workforce, [253] there is a pertinent need for India, at this stage, to take appropriate policy measures towards Iran through proper brinkmanship. Otherwise there is a distinct possibility that Iran will pronounce her tilt not only to Pakistan but also to an emerging Sino-Pak axis. If a step is taken by India towards an Iran-US rapprochement, it will not only produce the necessary balance but will also bring about two important results for India. First, it will further promote the on-going improvement in relations with the US; second, it will help India in addressing its own national interests as far as Iran is concerned. But how to orchestrate such an Iran-US rapprochement is a very difficult proposition, primarily because India has already lost the confidence of Iran. It can be revived only through proper, diplomatic and constructive manoeuvres, especially by interlocutors. Once that is effected, a step towards Iran-US rapprochement can be attempted. Hence, without spoiling more time and opportunity, it is crucial at this moment for the Indian policymakers to seriously ponder over these options and take actions in a strategic fashion.

NOTES AND REFERENCES

1   Peter Hopkirk, The Gr eat Game: On S ecret Service in High Asia, Oxf ord: Oxford University Press, 1990, pp. 1-07.

2   R.K.Ramazani, The F oreign P olicy of I ran, 1500-1941, Chalot tesville: University Press of Virginia, 1966, pp.89-90.

3   Sir A.W.Ward and G.P.Gooch, The Cambridge History of Bitish Foreign Policy, New York: 1923, pp. 320-321.

4   R.K.Ramazani, The Foreign Policy of Iran, 1500-1941, Chalottesvile:University Press of Virginia, 1966, pp.92-93.

5   Mohammad Reza Pahlavi, The Shah's Story: An Autobiography, (Translated from the French by Teresa Waugh), New Delhi: Vikas Publishing House Pvt. Ltd.,1980, pp.25-26

6   Quoted in R.K.R amazani, The F oreign P olicy of I ran, 1500-1941, Chalottesville:University Press of Virginia, 1966, p.141.

7   Quoted in R.K.R amazani, The F oreign P olicy of I ran, 1500-1941, Chalottesville:University Press of Virginia, 1966, p.144.

8   R.K.Ramazani, The Foreign Policy of Iran, 1500-1941, Chalottesvile:University Press of Virginia, 1966, pp.160-61.

9   R.K.Ramazani, The Foreign Policy of Iran, 1500-1941, Chalottesvile:University Press of Virginia, 1966, pp.229-230 and Mohammad Reza Pahlavi, The Shah's Story: An A utobiography, (Translated f rom the Fr ench by Teresa Waugh), New Delhi: Vikas Publishing House Pvt. Ltd., 1980, pp.41-42.

10   Kenneth M. Pollack, The Persian Puzzle, New Y ork: Random House, 2004, p.38.

11   Mohammad Reza Pahlavi, The Shah's Story: An Autobiography, (Translated from the French by Teresa Waugh), New Delhi: Vikas Publishing House Pvt. Ltd., 1980, pp.34-35.

12   Mohammad Reza Pahlavi, The Shah's Story: An Autobiography, (Translated from the French by Teresa Waugh), New Delhi: Vikas Publishing House Pvt. Ltd., 1980, p. 42.

13 William E. Gri ffith, "Iran's Foreign Policy in the P ahlavi Er a", in Geor ge Lenczowski (ed.), *Iran under the P ahlavis,* Cal ifornia: Hoo ver I nstitution Press, 1978, p.371; P atrick Clawson and Micheal Rubin, Eternal Ir an: Continuity and Chaos: New York, Palgrave Macmillan, 2005, p.58.

14 William E. Gri ffith, "Iran's Foreign Policy in the P ahlavi Er a", in Geor ge Lenczowski (ed.), *Iran under the P ahlavis,* Cal ifornia: Hoo ver I nstitution Press, 1978, p.371; P atrick Clawson and Micheal Rubin, *Eternal Ir an: Continuity and Chaos*: New York, Palgrave Macmillan, 2005, pp. 58-59.

15 Patrick Clawson and Micheal Rubin, *Eternal Iran: Continuity and Chaos* New York, Palgrave Macmillan, 2005, p.59.

16 Kenneth M. P ollack, *The Persian Puzzle*, New Y ork: Random House, 2004, pp.44-48; and Patrick Clawson and Micheal R ubin, *Eternal Iran: Continuity and Chaos*: New York, Palgrave Macmillan, 2005, pp. 59-60.

17 Patrick Clawson and Micheal Rubin, *Eternal Iran: Continuity and Chaos* New York, Palgrave Macmillan, 2005, p.60.

18 Patrick Clawson and Micheal Rubin, *Eternal Iran: Continuity and Chaos* New York, Palgrave Macmillan, 2005, p.62.

19 A.H.H. Abidi, *Relations between India and Ian, 1947-1979,* Occasional Paper, Gulf Studies   Programme, JNU, Delhi, p.4.

20 K R Singh, *Iran: Quest for Security*, New Delhi: Vikas Publishing House Pvt. Ltd, 1980, pp. 1-2.

21 Mohammad Reza Pahlavi, *The Shah's Story: An Autobiography,* (Translated from the French by Teresa Waugh), New Delhi: Vikas Publishing House Pvt. Ltd.,1980, p. 39.

22 Mohammad Reza Shah Pahlavi, *Mission of My country,* London, 1961, p.57.

23 K R Singh, *Iran: Quest for Security*, New Delhi: Vikas Publishing House Pvt. Ltd, 1980, pp. 3-4.

24 R. W. Cottam, *Nationalism in Iran,* University of Pittsburg Press, 1964, p.315.

25 R. W. Cottam, *Nationalism in Iran,* University of Pittsburg Press, 1964, p.314.

26 Text of Foreign Policy of India, Texts and Documents, 1947-1964, Lok Sabha Secretariat, 1966, New Delhi, p.42.

27 Ahmed Montaz eran and K ashif Mumtaz, "I ran-Pakistan: Cooper ation F or Regional Stability And P eace", available at ht tp://www.issi.org.pk/journal/ 2004_files/no_1/article/3a.htm

28 Text of Foreign Policy of India, Texts and Documents, 1947-1964, Lok Sabha Secretariat, 1966, New Delhi, p.43.

29   Text of Foreign Policy of India, Texts and Documents, 1947-1964, Lok Sabha Secretariat, 1966, New Delhi, pp.42-43..

30   SM. Burke, *Pakistan's Foreign Policy: An historical Analysis*, Karachi: Oxford University Press, 1990, p. 68.

31   Mujtaba Razvi, The Frontiers of Pakistan, Karachi: National Publishing House Ltd. 1971, p.203.

32   A.H.H. Abidi, *Relations between India and Iran, 1947-1979, Occasional Paper*, Gulf Studies   Programme, JNU, Delhi, p.5.

33   John Calabrese, *Revolutionary Horizons*, London: The Macmillan Press ltd. 1994, p.116.

34   Mujtaba Razvi, The Frontiers of Pakistan, Karachi: National Publishing House Ltd. 1971, pp.206-208.

35   Mujtaba Razvi, The Frontiers of Pakistan, Karachi: National Publishing House Ltd. 1971, p.208.

36   S.F.Hasnat, "Stagnating P akistan-Iran Relations", December 01, 2006, available at 2006, ht tp://www.chowk.com/articles/11418, accessed on 16 August 2010.

37   Mujtaba Razvi, The Frontiers of Pakistan, Karachi: National Publishing House Ltd. 1971, p.208

38   Mustafa Kibaroglu, "Iran's nuclear ambi tions from a historical perspectiv e and the attitude of the west ", *Middle Eastern Studies*, vol.43, no.2, March 2007, p. 223-224.

39   Mustafa Kibaroglu, "Iran's nuclear ambi tions from a historical perspectiv e and the attitude of the west ", *Middle Eastern Studies*, vol.43, no.2, March 2007, p. 223 and S.M. Burke, *Pakistan's Foreign Policy: An historical Analysis*, Karachi: Oxford University Press, 1990, p. 170.

40   *India:Lok Sabha Debates*, Vol.1, no.7, 25 March 1957, p.654.

41   Prithvi Ram Mudiam, *India and the Middle East*, London: British Academy Press, 1994, p.73.

42   See US-Iranian Relationship: A survey of US-Iranian Relations, 1941-1979, Top Secret, Report State, Digital National Security Archive, Item No.. IR03556, Washington, 29 January 1980, a   vailable at http:// www.nsarchive.chadwyck.com, accessed on April 01, 2010.

43   SM. Burke, *Pakistan's Foreign Policy: An historical Analysis*, Karachi: Oxford University Press, 1990, p. 171.

44   Mustafa Kibaroglu, "Iran's nuclear ambitions from a historical perspective and the attitude of the west", *Middle Eastern Studies*, vol.43, no.2, March 2007, p. 225.

45   Ayub Khan, *Friends not Masters*, Lahore: Oxford University Press, 1967, p. vii.

46   *Dawn,* 29 July 1964.

47   *Dawn*, 29 July 1964.

48   Noor Ul-haq(ed.), IPRI FACT FILE," Pakistan-Iran Relations", available at http://ipripak.org/factfiles/ff88.pdf

49   Rahimullah Yusufzai, "Pakistan-Afghan Relations: Hostage to the Past", *http://www.Cacianalyst.Org.*

50   Mujtaba Razvi, *The Frontiers of Pakistan*, Karachi: National Publishing House, 1971. p.210.

51   R.K.Ramazani, The Foreign Policy of Iran, 1500-1941, Chalottesvile:University Press of Virginia, 1966, p.266-268.

52   R.K.Amazani, The Foreign Policy of Iran, 1500-1941, Chalottesville:University Press of Virginia, 1966, p.272. See the detail text of the treaty in the Appendix.

53   Louis Dupree, "A Suggested Pakistan-Afghanistan-Iran Federation", *Middle East Journal,* Vol. 17, No. 4 (Autumn, 1963), pp. 383-387.

54   K. R. Singh,*Iran: Quest for Security*, New Delhi: Vikas Publshing House Pvt. Ltd, 1980, p.164.

55   John Calabese, *Revolutionary Horizons,* New York: St. Martin's Press, 1994, p.117.

56   Miron Rezun, "Iran and Afghanistan: With Specific Reference to their Asian Policies and Practices", *Journal of Asian and African Studies*, Vol.25, Nos. 1-2, 1990, p.23.

57   *Dawn*, 22 December 1955.

58   *Asian Recorder*, Vol. 2, 1956, p. 847.

59   Prithvi Ram Mudiam, *India and the Middle East* , London: British Academy Press, 1994, pp. 71-71.

60   *Dawn,* 10 May 1965.

61   SM. Burke, *Pakistan's Foreign Policy: An historical Analysis,* Karachi: Oxford University Press, 1990, p. 354.

62   Sushma Gupta, *Pakistan as a factor in Indo-Iranian Relations, 1947-1978*, New Delhi: Chand, 1988, p.93.

63   Khalida Qureshi*Pakistan and Iran-A study in neighbourly Diplomacy* Pakistan horizon, Karachi, vol. 21, No.1, First Quarter, 1968,p.38.

64   UN Official Records of the Gener al Assembly, 20th Session, 1362nd Plenary Meeting, 14 October 1965.

65   SM. Burke, *Pakistan's Foreign Policy: An historical Analysis*, Karachi: Oxford University Press, 1990, p. 354

66   SM. Burke, *Pakistan's Foreign Policy: An historical Analysis*, Karachi: Oxford University Press, 1990, p. 354

67   *Asian Recorder*, vol.14, no.34, 27 August-02 September 1966, p. 7254.

68   "Shah Reviews Foreign Policy", *Asian Recorder*, vol.12, no.33, 13-19 August 1966, p.7235.

69   K. R. Singh, *Iran: Quest for Security*, New Delhi: Vikas Publshing House Pvt. Ltd, 1980, pp. 166-167.

70   *The Statesman*, New Delhi, 9 May 1971.

71   K. R. Singh, *Iran: Quest for Security*, New Delhi: Vikas Publshing House Pvt. Ltd, 1980, p 167.

72   *The Times of India*, 16 September 1971.

73   *The Illustrated Weekly of India*, 10 October 1971.

74   Dawn, 15 December 1971.

75   K R Singh, *Iran: Quest for Security*, New Delhi: Vikas Publishing House Pvt. Ltd, 1980, p 168.

76   Quoted in K R Singh, *Iran: Quest for Security*, New Delhi: Vikas Publ ishing House Pvt. Ltd, 1980, p 169.

77   K R Singh, *Iran: Quest for Security*, New Delhi: Vikas Publishing House Pvt. Ltd, 1980, p 168-170.

78   Prithvi Ram Mudiam, *India and the Middle East*, London: British Academy Press, 1994, p. 107.

79   Amir Tahiri, "Policies of I ran in the P ersian gul f Region", in Abbas Ameri (ed.), *The Persian Gulf and the Indian Ocean in International Olitics,* Tehran: IPIS, 1975, PP.595-596.

80   K R Singh, *Iran: Quest for Security*, New Delhi: Vikas Publishing House Pvt. Ltd, 1980, pp.175.

81   See for details, K R Singh,*Iran: Quest for Security*, New Delhi: Vikas Publshing House Pvt. Ltd, 1980, pp.174-176; and Patrick Clawson and Michael Rubin, Eternal Iran, New York:Palgrave Macmillan, 2005, pp.82-84.

82   S.M. Burke, *Pakistan's Foreign Policy: An historical Analysis*, Karachi: Oxford University Press,   1990, p. 425.

83   S.M. Burke, *Pakistan's Foreign Policy: An historical Analysis*, Karachi: Oxford University Press, 1990, p. 426-27.

84   S.M. Burke, *Pakistan's Foreign Policy: An historical Analysis*, Karachi: Oxford University Press, 1990, p. 422.

85   S.M. Burke, *Pakistan's Foreign Policy: An historical Analysis,* Karachi: Oxford University Press,   1990, p. 426.

86   Prithvi Ram Mudiam, *India and the Middle East*, London: British Academy Press, 1994, pp. 76-77.

87   Prithvi Ram Mudiam, *India and the Middle East*, London: British Academy Press, 1994, pp. 76-77 and 108.

88   For details of Zias Islamisation process, see Lawrence Zairing, "From Islamic Republic to Islamic State in Pakistan", Asian Survey, vol-24, no.9, September 1984, pp.933-46; David Taylor, "The Politics of Islam and islamisation in Pakistan, in James Piscatori (ed.), *Islam in the Political process,* Cambridge: Cambridge university Press, 1983.

89   M.Hamid Ansari, "Introduction", in M H Ansari (ed), *Iran Today*, Delhi: Rupa and ORF, 2005, p.xi.

90   Ministry of foreign affairs, Islamic republic of Iran, http://www.mfa.gov.ir/ cms/cms/islamabad/en/PoliticalPart/Preface.html

91   See for details, Craig Baxter, "Pakistan and the Gulf", in Thomas Naff (ed.), *Gulf security and the Iran- Iraq War,* Washington D.C.: National Defence University Press, 1985, pp. 122-124.

92   US Department of State: "Diplomacy in action: Background Note, Iran", 23 July 2010, http://www.state.gov/r/pa/ei/bgn/5314.htm#relations, accessed on 12 October 2010

93   Kenneth M. Pollack, The Persian Puzzle, New York: Random House, 2004, pp.172-173.

94   Ali M. Ansari, *Confronting Iran,* New Delhi: Foundation Books, 2006, pp.86-87

95   During the Shah's reign, Iran had been Pakistan's second leading export market. During the 1980s,   Iran still ranked third. For details, Craig Baxter, "Pakistan becomes Prominent in the International arena", in Shahid Javed Burki and Craig Baxter (eds.), *Pakistan under the military regime*, Boulder: West view Press, 1991, p.146.

96   Shah Alam, "Iran-Pakistan Relations", *Strategic Analysis*, vol.28, no.4, Oct-Dec 2004, p.531.

97   "Pakistan's foreign economic relations", available at http://countrystudies.us/pakistan/47.htm accessed on 16 august 2010.

98   Ministry of foreign affairs, Islamic republic of iran, http://www.mfa.gov.ir/cms/cms/islamabad/en/PoliticalPart/Preface.html

99   Ministry of foreign affairs, Islamic republic of iran, http://www.mfa.gov.ir/cms/cms/islamabad/en/PoliticalPart/Preface.html

100   Ministry of foreign affairs, Islamic republic of iran,   htp://www.mfa.gov.ir/cms/cms/islamabad/en/PoliticalPart/Preface.html

101   Nasim Zehra, "Pakistan-Iran Relations: Compulsions and Condi tions for a Strategic Relationship", *Strategic Studies*, Vol. 23, no.1, spring 2003, pp. 76-89.

102   19 January 1994 , ht tp://www.nytimes.com/books/97/06/29/reviews/iran-transcript.html, accessed on 12 October 2010.

103   http://www.gwu.edu/~nsarchiv/NSAEBB/NSAEBB210

104   "The Iran-Contra Report". The American Pr esidency Pr oject. ht tp://www.presidency.ucsb.edu/PS157/assignment%20files%20public/congressional%20report%20key%20sections.htm. Retrieved 2008-05-17.

105   "Tower commission report excerpts". The Tower Commission Report. http:/www.presidency.ucsb.edu/PS157/assignment%20files%20public/TOWER%20EXCERPTS.htm. Retrieved 2008-06-07; and "R eagan's mixed White House legacy" . BB C. June 6, 2004. http://news.bbc.co .uk/2/hi/americas/213195.stm. Retrieved 2008-04-22.

106   "Tower commission report excerpts". The Tower Commission Report. http:/www.presidency.ucsb.edu/PS157/assignment%20files%20public/TOWER%20EXCERPTS.htm. Retrieved 2008-06-07.

107   "The Iran-Contra affair". The American-Israeli Cooperative Enterprise. http:/www.jewishvirtuallibrary.org/jsource/US-Israel/Iran_Contra_Affair.html. Retrieved 2008-06-07.

108   "Iran-Contra Report; Arms, Hostages and Contr as: How a S ecret Foreign Policy Unraveled" March 16, 1984. Retrieved on 2008-06-07

109   Hart, Robert (June 2, 2004). "NYT's apologies miss the point." The Consortium for Independent Journal ism, Inc. ht tp://www.consortiumnews.com/2004/060204.html. Retrieved 2008-06-07. and Gyeorgos C. Hatonn (1993). Chaparral Serendipity. Phoenix S ource Distributors, I nc.. p. 218. ISBN 9781569350003. http://books.google.com/books?id=alLIQuzswG8C.

110   http://www.gwu.edu/~nsarchiv/NSAEBB/NSAEBB210/14-Weinberger
       %20Diaries%20Dec%207%20handwritten.pdf

111   David Johnston (1991-10-20). "North Says Reagan Knew of Iran Deal". The
       New York Times. http://www.nytimes.com/1991/10/20/us/north-says-reagan-
       knew-of-iran-deal.html?pagewanted=1.

112   Ronald Reagan (November 13, 1986). "Address to the Nation on the I ran
       Arms and Contra Aid Controversy". Ronald Reagan Presidential Foundation.
       http://www.reagan.utexas.edu/archives/speeches/1986/111386c.htm.
       Retrieved 2008-06-07.

113   Ronald Reagan (1987-03-04). "Address to the Nation on the Iran Arms and
       Contra Aid Contr oversy". R onald R eagan Pr esidential Foundation. ht tp://
       www.reagan.utexas.edu/archives/speeches/1987/030487h.htm. R etrieved
       2008-06-07.

114   Ronald Reagan (November 13, 1986). "Address to the Nation on the I ran
       Arms and Contra Aid Controversy". Ronald Reagan Presidential Foundation.
       http://www.reagan.utexas.edu/archives/speeches/1986/111386c.htm.
       Retrieved 2008-06-07.

115   http://www.newsweek.com/2008/07/19/iran-s-nuclear-program.html,
       accessed on 01 December 2010.

116   Sharon Squassoni, "I ran's Nuclear Pr ogram: R ecent Dev elopments", CRS
       Report for Congress, Foreign Affairs, Defense, and Trade Division, Updated
       September 6, 2006http://www.fas.org/sgp/crs/nuke/RS21592.pdf

117   http://www.wordiq.com/definition/History_of_Iran, accessed 0n 06 December
       2010

118   Sharon Squassoni, "I ran's Nuclear Pr ogram: R ecent Dev elopments", CRS
       Report for Congress, Foreign Affairs, Defense, and Trade Division, Updated
       September 6, 2006http://www.fas.org/sgp/crs/nuke/RS21592.pdf

119   Sharon Squassoni, "I ran's Nuclear Pr ogram: R ecent Dev elopments", CRS
       Report for Congress, Foreign Affairs, Defense, and Trade Division, Updated
       September 6, 2006http://www.fas.org/sgp/crs/nuke/RS21592.pdf

120   Abbas Kadhim, "The future of nuclear weapons in the MiddleEast", in Peter
       R. Lavoy (ed), Nuclear Weapons Proliferation in the Next Decade, New York,
       Routledge, 2007. P151.

121   Abbas Kadhim, "The future of nuclear weapons in the MiddleEast", in Peter
       R. Lavoy (ed), Nuclear Weapons Proliferation in the Next Decade, New York,
       Routledge, 2007. P151.

122   http://www.oxfordresearchgroup.org.uk/oxford_research_group_
       chronology_irans_nuclear_programme_1957_2007

123   Mohammad Reza Pahlavi, The Shah's Story: An Autobiography, (Translated from the French by Teresa Waugh), New Delhi: Vikas Publishing House Pvt. Ltd., 1980, pp.67-68.

124   http://domino.un.org/unispal.nsf/0/43220e2368a3ddf 7052568000052412 c?OpenDocument and http://www .wsws.org/articles/2002/feb2002/sab-f22.shtml

125   http://www.time.com/time/magazine/article/0,9171,952421,00.html

126   Doughlas Brinkley (ed.), The Reagan Diaries. Washington DC: Harper Collns, 2007, pp. 87–90.

127   Gawdat Bahgat, "Nuclear Prolferation: The Islamic Republic of Iran", Iranian Studies, vol.39, no.3, September 2006, p.311.

128   Mitchell B.Reiss, "Without the Bomb: The Politics of nuclear non-prolferation, NewYork: Columbia university Press, 1988, p.83.

129   Rajesh Kumar Mishra, "Iranian Nuclear Programme and Pakistan", Strategic Analysis, Vol. 28, no. 3, 2004, p.441.

130   Implementation of the NPT Safeguards Agreement in the Islamic Republic of Iran: Report by Director General, IAEA, GOV/2003/75, No vember 26, 2003.p.19.

131   Tehran Home Service, January 12, 1985, BBC Monitoring, January 22, 1985, quoted in Ali M.Ansari, Confronting Iran, New Dlhi: Foundation Books, 2006, p.200.

132   Paul Kerr, "IAEA Presses to Iran to comply with Nuclear Safeguards", Arms Control Today, July/August 2003, pp.20-22.

133   Douglas Frantz, "Iran closes in on Ability to build a nuclear Bomb", The Los Angeles Times, A ugust 4, 2003. and Maggie F arley and B ob Dogrin, "Evi l behind the Axis", The Los Angeles Times, January 5, 2003.

134   Anwar Iqwal, "Father of Pakistan's Bomb in Trouble", The Washington Times, January 8, 2003. Also Maggie Farley and Bob Drogin, "Evil behind the Axis", The Los Angeles Times, January 5, 2003.

135   Youssef B odonsky, "P akistan's I slamic B omb", July 1998, a vailable at www.freeman.org.

136   Mustafa Kibar oglu, "Iran's nuclear ambi tions from a historical perspectiv e and the attitude of the west ", Middle Eastern Studies, vol.43, no.2, March 2007, p. 217-225.

137   Philip L. Ri tcheson, "Iranian Mi litary Resurgence: S cope, Motiv ations and Implications for Regional Security", Armed Forces and Society, Summer 1995, (21), p.4; Also see Kenneth R. Timmerman, "Weapons of Mass Destruction:

The cases of I ran, Syria and Lib ya, A Simon Wiesenthal Center Special Report, August 1992, pp . 41-42.; and also Wi lliam E. B urrows and R obert Windrem, *Critical Mass*, New York: Simon and Schuster, 1994, p.342.

[138]   Joby Warrick, "Nuclear Program in Iran Tied to Pakistan", *The Washington Post*, December 21, 2003, p .A01; Pakistan's Khan sold I ran Nuclear P arts, Police sa y, R euters, F ebruary 20, 2004; S onni Ef ron and Douglas Fr antz, "Secret Iran Nuclear Plan Discovered", *The Los Angeles Times*, February 13, 2004.

[139]   Rohan Sullivan, "Sources give details of Iran Nuke Deal", *The Washington Times*, February 20, 2004.

[140]   Browen Maddox, Iran admits Pakistan gave Key Nuclear Help", *The London Times,* November 13, 2003.

[141]   Jim Hoagland, "Biefing Yeltsin on Iran", *The Washington Post,* May 17, 1995, p.23.

[142]   Andew Koch, "Khanfessions of a Proliferator", *Janes Defence Weekly*, March 2004, 41(9), P.24.

[143]   Ehsan Ahrari, "Pakistan as Proliferator: A View from Washington", Asia Times Online. January 14 , 2003 at http://www.atimes.com/atimes/South_Asia/ EA14Df03.html and Job y W arrick, "I ran admi ts Foreign Help on Nuclear Facility", *The Washington Post*, August 27, 2003, p. A 17.

[144]   Douglas Frantz, "Iran closes in on Ability to build a nuclear bomb", *The Los Angeles Times*, August 4, 2003.

[145]   "Implementation of the NPT Safeguards Agreement in the Islamic Republic of Iran", Report by the Director General, Board of Governors, GOV/2003/63, September 12, 2003, p.6.

[146]   Mark Fitzpatrick, Lessons Learned f rom Iran's Pursuit of Nuclear Weapons, Peter R. Lavoy (ed), *Nuclear Weapons Proliferation in the Next Decade,* New York, Routledge, 2007. pp. 96-97.

[147]   Prithvi Ram Mudiam, *India and the Middle East,* London: British Academy Press, 1994, pp. 111-112.

[148]   Smruti S. Pattanaik, "Pakistan's Nuclear Str ategy", *Strategic Analysis*, Vol. 27, No. 1, Jan-Mar 2003,pp. 95-96.

[149]   Sumita kumar, "Pakistan-Iran Relations: The US F actor, *Strategic Analysis*, Vol. 32, No. 5, September 2008, p. 779

[150]   Interview with Khalid Mahmud, editor of the daily *Nation*, Lahore, Quoted in Vali Nasr, "The I ranian R evolution and Changes in I slamism in P akistan, India and Afghanistan", in Nikki R. Keddie and Rudi Matthee (eds.), Iran and

the surrounding world, Seattle and London: University of Washington Press, 2002), p.334

[151]   Vali Nasr, "The I ranian R evolution and Changes in I slamism in P akistan, India and Afghanistan", in Nikki R. Keddie and Rudi Matthee (eds.), Iran and the surrounding world, Seattle and London: University of Washington Press, 2002), pp.334-335

[152]   Vali Nasr, "The I ranian R evolution and Changes in I slamism in P akistan, India and Afghanistan", in Nikki R. Keddie and Rudi Matthee (eds.), Iran and the surrounding world, Seattle and London: University of Washington Press, 2002), pp.334-335

[153]   Vali Nasr, "The I ranian R evolution and Changes in I slamism in P akistan, India and Afghanistan", in Nikki R. Keddie and Rudi Matthee (eds.), Iran and the surrounding world, Seattle and London: University of Washington Press, 2002), pp.334-335

[154]   For details see Muhammad QasimZ aman, "S ectarianism in P akistan: The radicalization of Shi ia and Sunni identi ties", *Modern Asian studies*, vol.32, 1998, pp.687-716.

[155]   Sumita kumar, "Pakistan-Iran Relations: The US F actor, *Strategic Analysis*, Vol. 32, No. 5, September 2008, p. 777.

[156]   Sumita kumar, "Pakistan-Iran Relations: The US F actor, *Strategic Analysis*, Vol. 32, No. 5, September 2008, p. 778

[157]   Ilan Berman, *Tehran Rising*, London: Rowman and Litlefield Publishers, 2005, pp 46-47.

[158]   Ilan Berman, *Tehran Rising*, London: Rowman and Litlefield Publishers, 2005, pp 46-47.

[159]   Siddharth Varadarajan, "Iran and the invention of a nuclear crisis," The Hindu, Sep 21, 2005, http://www.hinduonnet.com/2005/09/21/stories/2005092105231000.htm

[160]   Lecture by Shyam Saran, the then Foreign Secretary of India, 'Nuclear Non-Proliferation and I nternational S ecurity', IDS A, I ndia Habi tat Centr e, New Delhi, October 24, 2005.

[161]   Robert S.Norris and Hans M. Kriestensen, "Pakistan's Nuclear Forces, 2007", *Bulletin of the Atomic Scientists,* Vol. 62, no.3, 2007, pp.71-73.

[162]   Lecture by Shyam Saran, the then Foreign Secretary of India, 'Nuclear Non-Proliferation and I nternational S ecurity', IDS A, I ndia Habi tat Centr e, New Delhi, October 24, 2005.

[163]   Ali M. Ansari, "I ran under Ahmadinejad" , Adelphi P aper 393, The Inteernational Institute for Strategic Studies, London, 2007, pp.11-12.

164   Kalim Bahadur, "Pakistani and Iranian Rivalry in Central Asia", *World Focus*, Vol.21, no.8, August 2000., pp.18-19.

165   "Perspective of Ties between the I.R.I ran and P akistan" ht tp:// www.iranembassy.pk/en/political-section/106-perspective-between.html, accessed on 30 September 2010.

166   Address by the Prime Mini tser to the I ranian Majl is, Tehran: November8, 1995, in Dr. Noor Ul Haq et al (eds.), *Pakistan-Iran Relations, IPRI Fact file* pp. 1-2, http://ipripak.org/factfiles/ff88.pdf

167   Abbas Maleki, "I   ran's R egional F oreign/Energy P olicy", www.caspianstudies.com, *accessed on 03 April 2010.*

168   Gulshan Dietl, "Iran and American W ars on its Plants" in M. Hamid Ansari (ed) *Iran Today,* Delhi: Rupa and Co., 2005, pp. 252-53.

169   http://wwwpakistan.gov.pk/ 12/26/2003, available at http://unpan1.un.org/ intradoc/groups/public/documents/apcity/unpan018848.pdf, ac cessed on April 01, 2010.

170   *Summary of World Broadcasts (SWB)*, BBC, December 10, 1999, Third Series ME/3714.

171   BBC, *SWB*, May 25, 1998, ME/3235.

172   BBC, *SWB*, May 25, 1998, ME/3235.

173   Asian Recorder, July 9–15, 1998, 44(28), p. 27417.

174   Asian Recorder, July 9–15, 1998, 44(28), p. 27417.

175   BBC, *SWB,* May 30, 1998, ME/3240.

176   Statement of I ran's Foreign Minister in I slamabad, a vailable in news f rom Russia, 1 December 2001, at http://newsfomrussia.com/world/2001/12/01/ 22651.html quoted in Dr. Noor ul Haq et al. (eds), *Pakistan-Iran Relations, IPRI Fact file*, p. 42, http://ipripak.org/factfiles/ff88.pdf

177   Statement of P akistan's F oreign Minister in I slamabad, a vailable in news from Russia, 1 December 2001, at http://newsfromrussia.com/world/2001/ 12/01/22651.html quoted in Dr . Noor ul Haq et al. (eds),   *Pakistan-Iran Relations, IPRI Fact file*, p. 44, http://ipripak.org/factfiles/ff88.pdf

178   Shar on Squassoni, "Iran's Nuclear Program: Recent Developments"; *CRS Report for Congress, Order Code RS21592,* Updated November 12, 2003, p.crs-1, av ailable at ht tp://www.parstimes.com/nuclear/crs_nov03.pdf, accessed on April 10, 2010.

179   ht tp://former.president.ir/khatami/eng/cronicnews/1381/8110/811004/ 811004.htm#b4

180   *Dawn*, 23 December 2002, ht tp://www.dawn.com/2002/12/23/top4.htm, available at Dr. Noor ul Haq et al. (eds), *Pakistan-Iran Relations, IPRI Fact file*, p. 49, http://ipripak.org/factfiles/ff88.pdf

181   Dawn, "Editorial", 27 December 2002, ht tp://www.dawn.com/2002/2002/12/27/ed.htm, quoted in Dr Noor ul Haq et al. (eds),*Pakistan-Iran Relations, IPRI Fact file*, p. 50, http://ipripak.org/factfiles/ff88.pdf

182   Ahmed Montazeran, *Kashif Mumtaz,* 'Iran-Pakistan: Cooperation For Regional Stability And Peace", http://www.issi.org.pk/journal/2004_files/no_1/article/3a.htm

183   Ali M. Ansari, "Iran under Ahmadinejad", *Adelphi Paper 393*, The International Institute for Strategic Studies, London, 2007, pp.41-42.

184   http://www2.irna.com/en/news/view/line-17/0705170716013844.htm

185   http://www2.irna.com/en/news/view/line-17/0705170716013844.htm.

186   http://www.irna.com/en/news/view/line-22/0612212936010042.htm

187   http://www.president.ir/eng/ahmadinejad/cronicnews/1384/07/01/index-e.htm,23 September 2005.

188   "Pakistan PM Seeks Wider Tade with Iran, Turkey," *Indo-Asian News Service*, November 11, 2007.

189   available at http://www.cbsnews.com/stories/2008/04/27/world/main4048570.shtml?source=RSSattr=HOME_4048570

190   "Zardari, Karzai, Ahmadinejad hold trlateral meeting", 11 March 2009, http://www.onepakistan.com/news/national/6454-iran-zardari-karzai-ahmadinejad-hold-trilateral-meeting.

191   "I ran, Pakistan Sign 4 MoUs on Mutual Cooper ation," *Fars News Agency*, June 30, 2008.

192   "Iran, P akistan Sign 4 MoUs on Mutual Cooper ation," *Fars News Agency*, June 30, 2008.

193   "Iran, Pakistan to Enhance T rade Volume by $1 Bn. ," *Fars News Agency*, June 27, 2008.

194   "Pakistan to Import 1,000 MW of Electricity from Iran," *Fars News Agency*, August 11, 2008.

195   http://www.apakistannews.com/iranian-ambassador-speaks-high-about-pakistan-iran-relations- 144870

196   "Iran Looks for Alies Through Asian and Latin American artnerships," *Power and Interest News Report*, November 27, 2007.

197   Girijesh Pant, *India: The Emerging Energy Player*, Delhi: Pearson Longman, 2008, p.139.

198   Gulshan Dietl, "Gas pipl ines: Politics and P ossibilities", in I.P. Khosla (ed), *Energy and Diplomacy*, New Delhi: K onark Publishers Pvt. Ltd., 2005, pp. 84-85.

199   Abbas Maleki, Iran's R egional F oreign/Energy P olicy, pp.07-08, www.caspianstudies.com, *accessed on 03 April 2010.*

200   Girijesh Pant, *India: The Emerging Energy Player*, Delhi: Pearson Longman, 2008, p.139.

201   Girijesh Pant, *India: The Emerging Energy Player*, Delhi: Pearson Longman, 2008, pp139-140

202   Amitav R anjan, "I ran Pipel ine: Now runs into US Sanctions" , The I ndian Express, 28 May 2003.

203   Girijesh Pant, *India: The Emerging Energy Player*, Delhi: Pearson Longman, 2008, p.142.

204   "IPI Pipeline Moves Ahead, Defying U.S " http://www.india-server.com/news/ipi-pipeline-moves-ahead-defying-u-s—3777.html, accessed on 01 December 2010

205   "Pakistan not intimidated b y US on pipel ine", 14 June 2005, ht tp:// forum.pakistanidefence.com/lofiversion/index.php/t45891.html, accessed on 01 December 2010.

206   *Tehran Times* , 30 Ma y 2010, http://www.tehrantimes.com/ index_View.asp?code=220359, accessed on 24 September 2010.

207   Patrick Goodenough, "I ran, Pakistan Push Ahead Wi th Gas Pipel ine Deal", *CNSNEWS.COM*, June 14, 2010, available on http://www.cnsnews.com/news/ article/67654

208   *Tehran Times* , 30 Ma y 2010, http://www.tehrantimes.com/ index_View.asp?code=220359, accessed on 24 September 2010.

209   *Tehran Times* , 30 Ma y 2010, http://www.tehrantimes.com/ index_View.asp?code=220359, accessed on 24 September 2010.

210   Patrick Goodenough, "I ran, Pakistan Push Ahead Wi th Gas Pipel ine Deal", CNSNEWS.COM, June 14, 2010, available on http://www.cnsnews.com/news/ article/67654

211   Patrick Goodenough, "I ran, Pakistan Push Ahead Wi th Gas Pipel ine Deal", June 14, 2010, http://www.cnsnews.com/news/article/67654

212   Mahan Abedin , "How to Defeat Jundal lah and Its Ilk" , http:// mrzine.monthlyreview.org/2009/abedin231009.html, 23-10-2009

[213] Michael Slackman, "I ran B lames U.S. and B ritain in A ttack", October 19, 2009; http://www. nytimes.com/2009/10/20/world/middleeast/20iran.htmlHello; "Iranian commanders assassinated", http://news.bbc.co.uk/2/hi/8312964.stm; and "Attack in I ran: What are the links to Pakistan?", October 18, 2009, EDThttp://blogs.reuters.com/pakistan/2009/10/18/attack-in-iran-what-are-the-links-to-pakistan, ACCESSED ON 18 October 2010.

[214] "Iran vows revenge after blast ki lls six Revolutionary Guards commanders and 37 others in Sistan-B aluchistan pr ovince", 18 October 2009, ht tp://www.guardian.co.uk/world/2009/oct/18/iran-suicide-bomb-revenge-vow

[215] Abubakar Siddique "Jundallah: Profile Of A Sunni Extremist Group", http://cejiss.org/online/jundallah/

[216] Sahar Zubairy , "Ir an Mourns" , October 21st 2009, http://iran.foreignpolicyblogs.com/tag/irgc/

[217] *Frontline,* Tehran B ureau, ht tp://www.pbs.org/wgbh/pages/frontline/tehranbureau/2009/10/jundallah.html, accessed on 18 October 2010

[218] "Jundallah: Ir an's Sunni rebels" , 20 Jun 2010, 11:25http://english.aljazeera.net/news/middleeast/2010/06/201062074140996374.html,accessed 0n 18 October 2010.

[219] "Suicide at tack tar geting I ran tr oops: Pr esident Mahmoud Ahmadinejad promises sharp retaliation", http://www.msnbc.msn.com/id/33366170/

[220] http://www.iaea.org/NewsCenter/Focus/IaeaIran/iaea_reports.shtml,

[221] http://www.france24.com/en/20090516-pakistan-afghanistan-iran-ahmadinejad-zardari-karzai- taliban-rebuilding.

[222] http://forum.pakistanidefence.com/lofiversion/index.php/t76210.html

[223] http://www.ecosecretariat.org/, accessed on 22 November 2010.

[224] http://www.ecosecretariat.org/, accessed on 22 November 2010.

[225] The group includes China, Kazakhstan, Kyrgyzstan, Russia, Tajikistan, and Uzbekistan as permanent members, and India, Iran, Mongolia, and Pakistan as observers.

[226] K.Omer, "Gwador: an emer ging gatew ay to Centr al Asia", *The News*, 22 April 2007, p.111.

[227] Roy Sultan Khan Bhatty, "Pakistan's Relations with the Central Asian Republics and the I mpact of Uni ted States' P olicies in Shaping R egional Dynamics", *Journal of S outh Asian and Middle Eastern Studies,* Vol. XXXII, No .1, Fall 2008, pp.78-79.

[228] K.Omer, "Gwador: an emer ging gatew ay to Centr al Asia", *The News*, 22 April 2007, p.111.

[229]   Ali Biniaz, "Prospects of Energy Cooperation between Iran and India: Case of the IPI Pipeline", p.111, in Meena Singh Roy(ed.), "INTERNATIONAL AND REGIONAL SECURITY DYNAMICS: Indian and Iranian Perspectives", IDSA, New Delhi, 2009.

[230]   *Pakistan Dail y*, 1 S   eptember 2010, ht   tp://www.daily.pk/ %E2%80%98ahmadinejad%E2%80%99s-visit-to-cement-ties%E2%80%99-21232/

[231]   *Kauthar:* An anthology of the speeches of Imam Khomeini, 1962-1978, Text of Speech number seventeen, Tehran: The Institute for the Compilation and Publication of the W orks of I mam Khomeini, p.181, also see http:// www2.irib.ir/worldservice/imam/speech/17.htm

[232]   Dr. Noor ul Haq et al. (eds), P akistan-Iran R elations, IPRI F act file, p. 3, http://ipripak.org/factfiles/ff88.pdf

[233]   Dr. Noor ul Haq et al. (eds), P akistan-Iran R elations, IPRI F act file, p. 3, http://ipripak.org/factfiles/ff88.pdf

[234]   Dr. Noor ul Haq et al. (eds), Pakistan-Iran Relations, IPRI Fact file, pp.9-10, http://ipripak.org/factfiles/ff88.pdf

[235]   *Foreign Affairs, Pakistan*, November-December 1995, pp.245-50, quoted inDr. Noor ul Haq et al. (eds), Pakistan-Iran Relations, IPRI Fact file, p. 62, available at http://ipripak.org/factfiles/ff88.pdf

[236]   "Iran's supreme leader backs Kashmir 'struggle", Indo-Asian News Service, Tehran, November 19, 2010 a vailable at ht tp://www.hindustantimes.com/ Iran-s-supreme-leader-backs-Kashmir-struggle/Article1-628346.aspx, accessed on 22 November 2010

[237]   Available at http://www.oic-oci.org/page_detail.asp?p_id=52, accessed on 06 October 2010

[238]   http://www.oic-un.org/oic_vienna_paris.asp

[239]   http://www.oic-un.org/index.asp

[240]   Isiaka Alani Badmus, The Vale of Tears: Kashmir, the Source of Indo-Pakistani Conflict Since 1947, Anthropologist, 8(2): 103-109 (2006)

[241]   M.Bhadra kumar "What Ir an did for India and why   it is hurt ", http:// www.rediff.com/news/2005/oct/03spec1.htm

[242]   http://en.wikipedia.org/wiki/Organisation_of_the_Islamic_Conference

[243]   http://en.wikipedia.org/wiki/Organisation_of_the_Islamic_Conference

[244]   http://en.wikipedia.org/wiki/Organisation_of_the_Islamic_Conference

[245]   Z.G. Muhammad, "Trouble in Kashmir's paradise", September 26, 2010 htp:/
/www.tehrantimes.com/index_View.asp?code=227357,tehran times, October
5, 2010

[246]   http://www.tehrantimes.com/index_View.asp?code=213262

[247]   Z.G. Muhammad, "Trouble in Kashmir's paradise", September 26, 2010 htp:/
/www.tehrantimes.com/index_View.asp?code=227357,tehran times, October
5, 2010

[248]   General Assembly of the   United Nations, ht tp://www.un.org/en/ga/65/
meetings/index.shtml

[249]   Pranab Dhal Samanta, "iran-slams-india-over-jandk-protests-india-hits-back",
Indian express, 5 October 2010, available at http://www.indianexpress.com/
news

[250]   http://rupeenews.com/2010/10/02/delhi-slaps-demarche-on-iran-over-
kashmir-criticism/ Tehran Times, Political Desk, 19 September 2010 http://
www.tehrantimes.com/index_View.asp?code=226896, ac cessed on 05
October 2010

[251]   http://www.indianexpress.com/news/iran-slams-india-over-j&k-protests-
india-hits-back-issues-demarche/691411/, accessed on 06 October 2010.

[252]   See the detai ls for such an emer ging axis BETWEEN I ran, P akistan and
China in K R Singh, " A new Axis: China, P akistan, Afghanistan and I ran",
Defence Watch, Vol.44, no.4, December 2010, pp14-18.

[253]   Address of the Hon'ble Vice President of India, Shri M. Hamid Ansari, at the
inauguration of the ICWA Conference titled "India and GCC Countries, I raq
and Iran: Emerging Security Perspectives" on 20 November 2010 at Gulmohar
Auditorium, India habitat Centre, New Delhi.

BIBLIOGRAPHY

GOVERNMENT DOCUMENTS: REPORTS/SPEECHES

Address by the Prime Minister of Pakistan to the Iranian Majlis, Tehran, 8 November 1995.

Ansari, M. Hamid, Address of the Vice President of India at the inauguration of the ICWA Conference titled *"India and GCC Countries, Iraq and Iran: Emerging Security Perspectives"* on 20 November 2010 at Gulmohar Auditorium, India habitat Centre, New Delhi.

An Anthology of the Speeches of Imam Khomeini, 1962-1978, KAUTHAR, Volumes: I-II-III, The Institute for the Compilation and Publication of the Works of Imam Khomeini, International Affairs Division, Tehran, Islamic Republic of Iran.

Bolton, John, "Iran's Continuing Pursuit of Weapons of Mass Destruction: Testimony by Under Secretary of State for Arms Control and International Security", House International Relations Committee, Subcommittee on the Middle East and Central Asia, 24 June 2004.

Central Intelligence Agency, "Iran under Rafsanjani: Seeking a new role in the World Community", October 1991, declassified, available at www.foia.cia.gov.accessed on 03 January 2011.

Central Intelligence Agency, "Russia-Iran: Planning Nuclear Power Cooperation", 19 March 1992, declassified, available at www.foia.cia.gov, accessed on 10 January 2011.

Central Intelligence Agency,"Persian Gulf: Bolder Iranian Actions", 30 September 1987, declassified, available at www.foia.cia.gov accessed on 24 December 2010.

Economy of Iran at a glance, New Delhi: Embassy of the Republic of Iran, 1997.

Foreign Policy of India, Texts and Documents, 1947-1964, Lok Sabha Secretariat, New Delhi, 1966.

Implementation of the NPT Safeguards Agreement in the Islamic Republic of Iran, Report by the Director General, Board of Governors, GOV/2003/63, September 12, 2003.

Implementation of the NPT Safeguards Agreement in the Islamic Republic of Iran, Report by Director General, IAEA, GOV/2003/75, November 26, 2003.

India: *Lok Sabha Debates*, Vol.1, no.7, 25 March 1957.

Katzman, Kenneth, "The Iran Sanctions Act (ISA)", CRS Report For Congress, Foreign Affairs, Defense, and Trade Division, Order Code Rs20871, Updated October 12, 2007,

http://www.fas.org/sgp/crs/row/RS20871.pdf, accessed on 20January 2011.

"Perspective of Ties between the I.R.Iran and Pakistan",Ministry of foreign affairs, Islamic republic of Iran, http://www.mfa.gov.ir/cms/cms/islamabad/en/PoliticalPart/Preface.html

Reagan, Ronald, (November 13, 1986). "Address to the Nation on the Iran Arms and Contra Aid Controversy". Ronald Reagan Presidential Foundation. http://www.reagan.utexas.edu/archives/speeches/1986/111386c.htm. Retrieved 2008-06-07.

Saran, Shyam, "Nuclear Non-Proliferation and International Security", Speech at India Habitat Centre, New Delhi, October 24, 2005.

Senate Foreign Relations Committee, "Iran and US policy: Testimony before the Senate Foreign Relations Committee", by Richard L. Armitage, Deputy Secretary of State, 28 October 2003.

Squassoni, Sharon, "Iran's Nuclear Program: Recent Developments", CRS Report for Congress, Foreign Affairs, Defense, and Trade Division, Updated September 6, 2006, http://www.fas.org/sgp/crs/nuke/RS21592.pdf.

Squassoni, Sharon, "Iran's Nuclear Program: Recent Developments"; *CRS Report for Congress, Order Code RS21592,* Updated November 12, 2003, p.crs-1, available at http://www.parstimes.com/nuclear/crs_nov03.pdf, accessed on April 10, 2010.

Statement of Iran's Foreign Minister in Islamabad, available in news from Russia, 1 December 2001, available at http://newsfromrussia.com/world/2001/12/01/22651.html, accessed on 20 December 2010.

Statement of Pakistan's Foreign Minister in Islamabad, available in news from Russia, 1 December 2001, at http://newsfromrussia.com/world/2001/12/01/22651.html

UN Official Records of the General Assembly, 20th Session, 1362nd Plenary Meeting, 14 October 1965.

US Department of State, "Excerpt: US, Iran Discussing Afghanistan, Iraq, Other issues of Mutual Interest", Press Release, 13 May 2003.

US Department of State: "Diplomacy in action: Background Note, Iran", 23 July 2010, http://www.state.gov/r/pa/ei/bgn/5314.htm#relations, accessed on 12 October 2010

US-Iranian Relationship: A survey of US-Iranian Relations, 1941-1979, Top Secret, Report State, Digital National Security Archive, Item No.. IR03556, Washington, 29 January 1980, available at http://www.nsarchive.chadwyck.com, accessed on April 01, 2010.

BOOKS/MONOGRAPHS:

Abidi, A.H.H., *Relations between India and Iran, 1947-1979,* Occasional Paper, Gulf Studles Programme, JNU, Delhi.

Abrahamian, Ervand, *Iran between two Revolutions,* Princeton: Princeton University Press, 1982.

Abrahamian, Ervand, *Khomeinism: Essays on the Islamic Republic,* London: I.B.Tauris, 1993.

Adib-Moghaddam, Arshin, *Iran in World Politics,* London: Hurst and Company, 2007.

Adib-Moghaddam, Arshin, *The International Politics of the Persian Gulf*, New York: Routledge, 2006.

Afrasiabi, Kaveh L., *After Khomeini: New Directions in Iran's Foreign Policy*, Boulder: Westview, 1994.

Akhavi, Shahrough, *Religion and politics in contemporary Iran*, Albany, State University of New York Press,1980.

Al- Suwaidi, Jamal S., *Iran and the Gulf: A search for stability,* Abu Dhabi: ECSSR, 1996.

Ameri, Abbas (ed.), *The Persian Gulf and the Indian Ocean in International Politics,* Tehran: IPIS, 1975.

Amirahmadi, Hooshang and Nader Entessar (eds.), *Iran and the Arab World*, London: MacMillan, 1993.

Amirasadeghi, Hossein, (ed.), *The Security of the Persian Gulf*, London: Croom helm, 1991.

Ansari, Ali M, *Confronting Iran:The Failure of American Foreign policy and the roots of Mistrust,* New Delhi: Foundation Books, 2006.

Ansari, Ali M, *Iran under Ahmadinejad,* Adelphi Paper 393, The International Institute for Strategic Studies, London, 2007.

Ansari, M H, (ed.), *Iran Today*, Delhi: Rupa and ORF, 2005.

Arjomand, Said A., *The Turban and the Crown,* New York: Oxford University Press, 1988.

Atabaki, Touraj, *Iran and the First World War,* London: I B Tauris, 2005.

Baker, James A. III, *The Politics of Diplomacy,* New York: G.P. Putnam's Sons, 1995.

Bakhash, Shaul, *The Reign of the Ayatollahs: Iran and the Islamic Revolution*, New York: Basic Books, 1990.

Berman, Ilan, *Tehran Rising*, London: Rowman and Littlefield Publishers, 2005

Bill, James A, *The Eagle and the Lion: The Tragedy of American-Iranian Relations*, New Haven, Conn.: Yale University Press, 1988.

Brinkley, Doughlas (ed.), *The Reagan Diaries,* Washington DC: Harper Collins, 2007.

Brumberg, Daniel, *Reinventing Khomeini: The Struggle for Reform in Iran*, Chicago: University of Chicago Press, 2001.

Brzezinski, Zbigniew, *Power and Principle: Memoirs of the National Security Adviser, 1977-1981,* New York: Farrar, Straus and Giroux, 1985.

Buchta, Wilfried, Who Rules Iran? The Structure of Power in the Islamic Republic, Washington, D.C.: Washington Institute for Near East Policy and the Konrad Adenauer Stiftung, 2000.

Bulloch, John and Harvey Morris, *The Gulf War*, London: Methuen, 1989.

Burke, S.M., *Pakistan's Foreign Policy: An historical Analysis*, Karachi: Oxford University Press, 1990.

Burki , Shahid Javed and Craig Baxter (eds.), *Pakistan Under The Military Regime*, Boulder: West view Press, 1991.

Burrows, William E and Robert Windrem, *Critical Mass*, New York: Simon and Schuster, 1994.

Calabrese, John, *Revolutionary Horizons*, London: The Macmillan Press ltd. 1994

Carter, Jimmy, *Keeping Faith: Memoirs of a President*, Fayetteville, Ark.: University of Arkansas Press, 1995.

Christopher, Warren and Paul H. Kreisberg(ed.), *American Hostages in Iran: The Conduct of a Crisis,* New Haven, Conn.: Yale University Press, 1985.

Chubin, Shahram and Charles Tripp, *Iran and Iraq at War,* London: I BTauris, 1988.

Chubin, Shahram, *Iran's National Security Policy: Capabilities, Intentions, and Impact*, Washington, D.C: Carnegie Endowment, 1994.

Clawson, Patrick and Michael Rubin, *Eternal Iran*, New York: Palgrave Macmillan, 2005.

Cottam, R. W., *Nationalism in Iran,* University of Pittsburg Press, 1964.

Daniel, Elton L, *The History of Iran*, Westport, Conn.: Greenwood Press, 2001.

Ebtekar, Massoumeh, *Takeover in Tehran: The Inside Story of the 1979 US Embassy Capture,* Vancouver, Canada: Talon Books, 2000.

Ehteshami, Anoushiravan and Mahjoob Zweiri, *Iran and the Rise of Neo-conservatives,* London: IBTauris, 2007.

Ehteshami, Anoushiravan, *After Khomeini: The Iranian Second Republic.* London: Routledge, 1995.

Eisenstadt, Michael, *Iranian Military Power: Capabilities and Intentions,* Washington, D.C.: Washington Institute for Near East Policy, 1997.

Esposito, John L., (ed.), *The Iranian Revolution: Its Global Impact*, Gainsville: University Press of Florida, 1990.

Esposito, John L., and R.K. Ramazani (eds.), *Iran at the Crossroads,* New York: Palgrave, 2001.

Fischer, Michael M, *Iran: From Religious Dispute to Revolution*, Madison: University of Wisconsin Press, 1980.

Fuller, Graham E, *The Center of the Universe: The Geopolitics of Iran,* Boulder, Colo.: West view, 1991.

Garver, John W., *China and Iran*, London: university of Washington press, 2006.

Gasiorowski, Mark J, *US. Foreign Policy and the Shah: Building a Client State in Iran,* Ithaca, N.Y.: Cornell University Press, 1991.

Ghani, Cyrus, *Iran and the rise of Reza Shah*, London: I B Tauris, 1998.

Gheissari, Ali and Vali Nasr, *Democracy in Iran*, New York: Oxford University Press, 2006.

Gieling, Saskia, *Religion and War in Revolutionary Iran*, London: I. B. Tauris, 1999.

Glantz, David M., and Jonathan House, *When Titans Clashed: How the Red Army Stopped Hitler,* Lawrence, Kans.: University of Kansas Press, 1995.

Gonzalez, Nathan, *Engaging Iran,* Westport: Praeger Security International, 2007.

Grover, Verinder and Ranjana Arora, (eds.), *Political System in Pakistan*, New Delhi; Deep & Deep Publications, New Delhi, 1995

Gupta, Sushma, *Pakistan as a factor in Indo-Iranian Relations, 1947-1978*, New Delhi: Chand, 1988.

Halliday, Fred, *Iran: Dictatorship and Development*, London: Penguin Books, 1979.

Hashim, Ahmed, *The Crisis of the Iranian State, Adelphi Paper no. 296*, London: IISS, 1995.

Hiro, Dilip, *The Longest War: The Iran-Iraq Military Conflict*, New York: Routledge, 1991.

Houghton, David Patrick, *US Foreign Policy and the Iran Hostage Crisis*, Cambridge, U.K.: Cambridge University Press, 2001.

Huyser, General Robert E, *Mission to Tehran*, New York: Harper and Row, 1986.

Isaacson, Walter, *Kissinger: A Biography*, New York: Touchstone, 1992.

Jafarzadeh, Alireza, *Iran Threat*, New York: Palgrave Macmillan, 2007.

Jaffrelot, Christophe, (ed.), *A History of Pakistan*, Paris: Anthem Press, 2002.

Katouzian, Homa (ed.), *Iran in the twenty-first century*, London: Routledge, 2008.

Katouzian, Homa, *State and Society in Iran,* London: IBTauris, 2001.

Keddie, Nikki R, *Modern Iran: Roots and Results or Revolution*, New Haven, Conn.: Yale University Press, 2003.

Keddie, Nikki R. and Rudi Matthee (eds.), *Iran and the surrounding world*, Seattle and London: University of Washington Press, 2002.

Kemp, Geoffrey, (ed.), *Iran's Nuclear Weapons Options: Issues and Analysis*, Washington, D.C.: Nixon Center, 2001.

Kemp, Geoffrey, *US and Iran: The Nuclear Dilemma: Next Steps,* Washington, D.C.: Nixon Center, 2004.

Khan, Ayub, *Friends not Masters*, Lahore: Oxford University Press, 1967,

Khatami, Mohammad, *Islam, Dialogue and Civil Society*, Canberra: Centre for Arab and Islamic Studies, The Australian National University, 2000.

Khomeini, Ruhollah, *Islam and Revolution: Writings and Declarations of Imam Khomeini*, translated and annotated by Hamid Algar, Berkeley: Mizan, 1981.

Kissinger, Henry, *White House Years*, Boston: Little, Brown, 1979.

Kissinger, Henry, *Years of Renewal*, London: Weidenfeld and Nicolson, 1999.

Kissinger, Henry, *Years of Upheaval*, London: Weidenfeld and Nicolson, 1982.

Kornbluh, Peter, and Malcolm Byrne, *The Iran-Contra Scandal: The Declassified History,* New York: W.W. Norton, 1993.

Kuniholm, Bruce, *The Origins of the Cold War in the Near East: Great Power Conflict and Diplomacy in Iran, Turkey and Greece*, Princeton, N.J: Princeton University Press, 1980.

Kurzman, Charles, *The Unthinkable Revolution in Iran,* Cambridge, Mass.: Harvard University Press, 2004.

Lavoy, Peter R. (ed), *Nuclear Weapons Proliferation in the Next Decade*, New York, Routledge, 2007. pp. 96-97.

Lenczowski , George (ed.), *Iran Under the Pahlavis*, California: Hoover Institution Press, 1978.

Litwak, Robert S, *Rogue States and U.S. Foreign Policy*, Washington, D.C.: Woodrow Wilson Center, 2000.

Mafinejam, Alidad and Aria Mehrabi, *Iran and its Place among nations,* Westport:Praeger, 2008.

Malcolm Byrne and Mark J. Gasiorowski (eds.), *Mohammad Mosaddeq and the 1953 Coup in Iran,* Syracuse, N.Y.: Syracuse University Press, 2004.

Marschall, Christin, *Iran's Persian Gulf policy: From Khomeini to Khatami*, London: Routledge Curzon, 2003.

Martin, Vanessa, *Creating an Islamic Stale: Khomeini and the Making of a New Iran*, London: I. B. Tuuris, 2000.

Menashri, David, *A Decade of War and Revolution,* New York: Holmes and Meier, 1990.

Menashri, David, *Post-Revolutionary politics in Iran*, London: Frank Cass, 2001.

Metz, Helen Chapin, *Iran: A Country Study,* Washington, D.C.: US. Government Printing Office, 1989.

Moslem, Mehdi, *Factional Politics in Post-Khomeini Iran*, Syracuse, N.Y: Syracuse University Press, 2002.

Mottahedeh, Roy, *The Mantle of the Prophet: Religion and Politics in Iran*, New York: Pantheon, 1985.

Mottale, Morris M, *Iran: The Political Sociology of the Islamic Revolution*, Lanham: University Press of America, 1995.

Mudiam, Prithvi Ram, *India and the Middle East*, London: British Academy Press, 1994.

Pahlavi, Mohammad Reza Shah, *Mission of My country*, London, 1961.

Pahlavi, Mohammad Reza Shah, *The Shah's Story: An Autobiography,* (Translated from the French by Teresa Waugh), New Delhi: Vikas Publishing House Pvt. Ltd., 1980,

Palmer, Michael A, *Guardians of the Gulf: A History of America's Expanding Role in the Persian Gulf, 1833-1992*, New York: Free Press, 1992.

Pant, Girijesh, *India: The Emerging Energy Player,* Delhi: Pearson Longman, 2008.

Parsons, Anthony, *The Pride and the Fall, Iran: 1974-1979,* London: Jonathan Cape, 1984.

Pasha, A.K., *India, Iran and the GCC States: Political Strategy and Foreign Policy*, New Delhi: Manas Publishers, 2000.

Pelletiere, Stephen, *The Iran-Iraq War,* New York: Praeger, 1992.

Pelmani, Hooman, *Iran and the United States: The rise of the West Asian Regional Grouping,* London: Praeger, 1999.

Piscatori, James (ed.), *Islam in the Political process,* Cambridge: Cambridge University Pre

Pollack, Kenneth M., *The Persian Puzzle,* New York: Random House, 2004ss, 1983.

Prasad, Bimal, *Origins of India's Foreign Policy*, Calcutta, 1960.

Ramazani, Ruhollah K, *Iran's Foreign Policy, 1941-73,* Chalottesville: University Press of Virginia, 1975.

Ramazani, Ruhollah K, *The Foreign Policy of Iran, 1500-1941*, Chalottesville: University Press of Virginia, 1966.

Ramazani, Ruhollah K.(ed.), *Iran at the Crossroads*, Houndmills: Palgrave, 2001.

Ramazani, Ruhollah K., *Revolutionary Iran*, Baltimore, John Hopkins, 1986.

Ramazani, Ruhollah K., *The Persian Gulf: Iran's Role,* Charlottesville: University of Virginia Press, 1972.

Razvi, Mujtaba, *The Frontiers of Pakistan*, Karachi: National Publishing House Ltd. 1971.

Reiss, Mitchell B, *Without the Bomb: The Politics of nuclear non-proliferation*, NewYork: Columbia university Press, 1988.

Schake, Kori N" and Judith S, Yaphe, *The Strategic Implications of a Nuclear Armed Iran,* McNair Paper 64. Washington, D.C.: National Defense University, 2001.

Shultz, George P, *Turmoil and Triumph*, New York: Charles Scribner's Sons. 1993.

Sick, Gary, *All Fall Down: America's Fateful Encounter with Iran*, London: I. B. Tauris. 1985.

Singh, K R, *Iran: Quest for Security*, New Delhi: Vikas Publishing House Pvt. Ltd, 1980.

Sullivan, William H, *Mission to Iran*, New York: W.W. Norton, 1981.

Tanter, Raymond, *Rogue Regimes: Terrorism and Proliferation*, New York: St. Martin's Griffin, 1999.

Tarock, Adam, *Iran's Foreign Policy since 1990*, Commack: Nova Science, 1999.

Thomas Naff (ed.), *Gulf security and the Iran- Iraq War*, Washington D.C.: National Defence University Press, 1985, pp. 122-124.

Vance, Cyrus. *Hard Choices: Critical Years in America s Foreign Policy*, New York: Simon & Schuster, 1983.

Weinberger, Caspar, *Fighting for Peace*, New York: Warner Books, 1990.

Wells, Tim, *444 Days: The Hostages Remember,* New York: Harcourt Brace Jovanovich, 1985.

Wright, Robin, *In the Name of God: The Khomeini Decade*, New York: Simon & Schuster, 1999.

Wright, Robin, *The Last Great revolution*, New York: Vintage Books, 2001.

Zak, Chen, *Iran's Nuclear Policy and the IAEA,* Washington, D.C.: Washington institute of Neareast policy, 2002.

ARTICLES IN BOOKS AND JOURNALS

Ahmad, Talmiz, "Iran-Pakistan-india Gas Pipeline", *Seminar,* No.584, April 2008, pp.48-51.

Alam, Shah, "Iran-Pakistan Relations", *Strategic Analysis,* vol.28, no.4, Oct-Dec 2004, pp.526-545.

Ansari, Ali M., "Continuous Regime Change from Within", *The Washington Quarterly,* Autumn 2003, pp.53-67.

Badmus, Isiaka Alani , "The Vale of Tears: Kashmir, the Source of Indo-Pakistani Conflict Since 1947", *Anthropologist,* Vol.8, No.2, 2006, pp.103-109

Bahadur, Kalim, "Pakistani and Iranian Rivalry in Central Asia", *World Focus*, Vol.21, no.8, August 2000, pp.18-20.

Bahgat, Gawdat, "Nuclear Proliferation: The Islamic Republic of Iran", *Iranian Studies,* vol.39, no.3, September 2006, p.311.

Barzegar, Kayhan, "Understanding the Roots of Iranian Foreign policy in the New Iraq", *Middle East Policy*, Vol.XII, No.2, Summer 2005, pp.49-77.

Baxter, Craig, "Pakistan and the Gulf", in Thomas Naff (ed.), *Gulf security and the Iran- Iraq War,* Washington D.C.: National Defence University Press, 1985, pp. 122-124.

Behrooz, Maziar, "Trends in the Foreign Policy of the Islamic Republic of Iran, 1979-1988." in Nikki R. Keddie and Mark J. Gasiorowski (ed.),

Neither East nor West: Iran, the Soviet Union, and the United States, New Haven, Conn.: Yale University Press, 1990, pp. 13-35.

Bellaigue, Christopher, "Iran's Last Chance for Reform", *The Washington Quarterly* 24, no. 4, Autumn 2001, pp.71-80.

Bhandari, Romesh, "Pakistan and the Region", *World Focus*, Vol.30, No.4, April 2009, pp.145-149.

Bhatty, Roy Sultan Khan, "Pakistan's Relations with the Central Asian Republics and the Impact of United States' Policies in Shaping Regional Dynamics", *Journal of South Asian and Middle Eastern Studies,* Vol. XXXII, No.1, Fall 2008, pp.78-79.

Bill, James A, "Modernization and Reform from Above: The Case of Iran." *The Journal of Politics Vol.* 32, no. 1, February 1970, pp.19-40.

Biniaz, Ali, "Prospects of Energy Cooperation between Iran and India: Case of the IPI Pipeline", in Meena Singh Roy (ed.), *International and Regional Security Dynamics: Indian and Iranian Perspectives*, IDSA, New Delhi, 2009.

Burgess, C, William H. III, "Special Operations in the Iran-Iraq War." *Special Warfare*, Winter 1989, pp. 16-29.

Byrne, Malcolm, "The Road to Intervention: Factors Influencing U.S. Policy Toward Iran. 1945-1953", in Malcolm Byrne and Mark J. Gasiorowski(ed.), *Mohammad Mosaddeq and the 1953 Coup in Iran,* Syracuse, N.Y.: Syracuse University Press, 2004, pp. 201-226.

Campbell, John C, "Oil Power in the Middle East", *Foreign Affairs* Vol.56, no. I, October 1977, pp. 89-110.

Carswell, Robert and Richard J. Davis, "Crafting the Financial Settlement." in Warren

Chandra, Satish, "Pakistan-Afghanistan Situation", *Indian Foreign Affairs Journal*, Vol.4, No.3, July-September 2009, pp.01-32.

Chowdhury, M.S., "Pakistan's Strategic Depth", *USI Journal*, Vol. 139, No.577, September 2009, pp. 345-354.

Christopher and Paul H. Kreisberg (ed.), *American Hostages in Iran: The Conduct of a Crisis,* New Haven, Conn.: Yale University Press, 1985, pp. 201-234.

Chubin, Shahram and Robert S. Litwak, "Debating Iran's Nuclear Aspirations", *The Washington Quarterly,* Autumn 2003, pp.99-114.

Chubin, Shahram, "Iran's Security in the 1980s", *International Security* Vol.2, no. 3, Winter 1978, pp. 51-80.

Cooper, Andrew Scott, "Showdown at Doha: The Secret Oil Deal that Helped Sink the Shah of Iran", *Middle East Journal,* Vol.62, No.4, Autumn 2008, pp.567-592.

Cornell, Svante E, "Iran and the Caucasus", *Middle East Policy* Vol.5, no. 4, January 1998.

Cottrell, Alvin, "Iran's Armed Forces Under the Pahlavi Dynasty." in George Lenczowski (ed.), *Iran Under the Pahlavis,* Stanford, California: Hoover Institution Press, 1978, pp. 389-431.

Dadkhah, Karnran M, "The Inflationary Process of the Iranian Economy, 1970-1980." *International Journal of Middle East Studies*, Vol.17, no. 3, August 1985, pp. 365-381.

David Taylor, "The Politics of Islam and Islamisation in Pakistan", in James Piscatori (ed.), *Islam in the Political process*, Cambridge: Cambridge university Press, 1983.

Dietl, Gulshan, "Gas piplines: Politics and Possibilities", in I.P. Khosla (ed), *Energy and Diplomacy,* New Delhi: Konark Publishers Pvt. Ltd., 2005, pp. 84-85.

Dietl, Gulshan, "Iran and American Wars on its Plants" in M. Hamid Ansari (ed.), *Iran Today,* Delhi: Rupa and Co., 2005, pp. 252-53.

Dupree, Louis, "A Suggested Pakistan-Afghanistan-Iran Federation", *Middle East Journal,* Vol. 17, No. 4, Autumn, 1963, pp. 383-387.

Einhorn, Robert J. and Gary Samore, "Ending Russian Assistance to Iran's Nuclear Bomb", *Survival* , Vol.44, no. 2, Summer 2002, pp. 51-70.

Eisenstadt, Michael, "Iran's Nuclear Program: Gathering Dust or Gaining Steam?" *Policy Watch no. 707*, Washington Institute for Near East Policy, February 2003.

Eldin, Fred S, "On the Road: Coping in Islamic Iran", *Middle East Quarterly*, June 1997.

Entessar, Nader, "Iran's Nuclear Decision-Making Calculus", *Middle East Policy*, Vol.XVI, No.2, Summer 2009, pp.26-38.

Fair, C Christine, "Pakistan's Relations with Central Asia", *Journal of Strategic Studies,* Vol. 31, No.2, April 2008, pp. 201-227.

Fairbanks, Stephen C, "A New Era for Iran?" *Middle East Policy,* Vol. 5, no. 3, September 1997, pp. 51-57.

Farhi, Farideh, "To Have or Not to Have? Iran's Domestic Debate on Nuclear Weapons" in Geoffrey Kemp (ed.), *Iran's Nuclear Weapons Options: Issues and Analysis*, Washington, D.C.: Nixon Center, 2001, pp. 35-53.

Freedman, Robert, "Russian-Iranian Relations in the 1990s", *MERIA Journal* Vol. 4, No. 2, June 2000.

Gasiorowski, Mark J. "The 1953 Coup d'etat against Mosaddeq", in Malcolm Byrne and Mark Gasiorowski (ed.), *Mohammad Mosaddeq and the 1953 Coup in Iran*, Syracuse, N.Y.: Syracuse University Press, 2004, pp. 227-260.

Griffith, William E, "Iran's Foreign Policy in the Pahlavi Era", in George Lenczowski (ed.), *Iran Under the Pahlavis,* Stanford, California: Hoover Institution Press, 1978, pp. 365-388.

Hanson, Brad, "The 'Westoxication' of Iran", *International Journal of Middle East Studies,* Vol.15, No.1, February 1983, pp.1-23.

Heiss, Mary Ann, "The International Boycott of Iranian Oil and the Anti-Mosaddeq Coup of 1953", in Malcolm Byrne and Mark J. Gasiorowski (ed.), *Mohammad Mosaddeq and the 1953 Coup in Iran,* Syracuse, N.Y.: Syracuse University Press, 2004, pp. 178-200.

Hooglund, Eric, "The Gulf War and the Islamic Republic", *MERIP Middle East Report* July-September 1984, pp. 125-126.

Jawdat, Nameer Ali, "Reflections on the Gulf War", *Arab-American Affairs*,Vol. 5 Summer 1983.

Kanovsky, Eliyahu. "Iran's Sick Economy: Prospects for Change Under Khatami", in Patrick Clawson (ed.), *Iran Under Khatami,* Washington, D.C.: Washington Institute for Near East Policy, 1998.

Kasturi, Bhashyam, "Pakistan's Second Front", *Agni*, Vol.9, No. 4, October-December 2006, pp.66-73.

Katouzian, Homa, "The Aridisolatic Society: A Model of Long- Term Social and Economic Development in Iran", *International Journal of Middle East Studies* Vol.15, no. 2, May 1983, pp. 259-281.

Katz, Mark, "Russian-Iranian Relations in the Ahmadinejad Era", *Middle East Journal,* Vol.62, No.2, Spring 2008, pp.202-216.

Kennedy, Edward M, "The Persian Gulf: Arms Race or Arms Control." Foreign Affairs 54, no. I (October 1975): 14-35.

Kerr, Paul, "IAEA Presses to Iran to comply with Nuclear Safeguards", *Arms Control Today,* July/August 2003, pp.20-22.

Kibaroglu, Mustafa,"Iran's nuclear ambitions from a historical perspective and the attitude of the West", *Middle Eastern Studies*, Vol.43, no.2, March 2007, pp. 223-245.

Koch, Andrew,"Khanfessions of a Proliferator", *Janes Defence Weekly*, Vol.41, No.9, March 2004.

Kumar, Sumita,"Pakistan-Iran Relations: The US Factor", *Strategic Analysis*, Vol. 32, No. 5, September 2008, pp. 773-789.

Ladjevardi, Habib, "The Origins of US. Support for an Autocratic Iran", *International Journal of Middle East Studies,* Vol. 15, no. 2, May 1983, pp. 225-239.

Lake, Anthony, "Confronting Backlash States", *Foreign Affairs* Vol.73, no. 2, March-April 1994.

Levy, Walter, "Issues in International Oil Policy", *Foreign Affairs*, April 1957, pp. 454-469.

Lilienthal, David E, "Enterprise in Iran: An Experiment in Economic Development", *Foreign Affairs*, October 1959, pp. 132-139.

Malik, Mustafa, "Pakistan", *Middle East Policy*, Vol.16, No.2, Summer 2009, pp.138-148.

Mark Fitzpatrick, "Lessons Learned from Iran's Pursuit of Nuclear Weapons", Peter R. Lavoy (ed), *Nuclear Weapons Proliferation in the Next Decade*, New York: Routledge, 2007, pp. 96-97.

Mishra, Rajesh Kumar, "Iranian Nuclear Programme and Pakistan", *Strategic Analysis,* Vol. 28, No. 3, 2004, pp.440-453.

Mohammadi-Nejad, Hassan, "The Iranian Parliamentary Elections of 1975", *International Journal of Middle East Studies*, Vol. 8, no. I (January 1977): 103-116.

Mohammed, Nadeya Sayed Ali, "Political Reform in Bahrain: The Price of Stability", *Middle East Intelligence Bulletin* 4, 110. 9 (September 2002).

Morocco, John, et al, "Iranian Airbus Shootdown", *Aviation Week and Space Technology* 129, no. 2 (July 11, 1988): 16.

Muhammad QasimZaman, "Sectarianism in Pakistan: The Radicalization of Shiia and Sunni identities", *Modern Asian Studies*, Vol.32, 1998, pp.687-716.

Nasr, Vali, "The Iranian Revolution and Changes in Islamism in Pakistan, India and Afghanistan", in Nikki R. Keddie and Rudi Matthee (eds.), *Iran And The Surrounding World,* Seattle and London: University of Washington Press, 2002, pp.334-335.

Norris, Robert S and Hans M. Kriestensen, "Pakistan's Nuclear Forces, 2007", *Bulletin of the Atomic Scientists,* Vol. 62, no.3, 2007, pp.71-73.

Paine, Chris and Erica Schoenberger, "Iranian Nationalism and the Great Powers, 1872-1954", *MERIP Reports* 37 (May 1975): 3-28.

"Pakistan's Foreign policy: Quarterly Survey", *Pakistan Horizon*, Vol.57, No.4, October 2004, pp.1-24.

Parasiliti, Andrew, "Iran: Diplomacy and Deterrence", *Survival*, Vol. 51, No.5, October-November 2009, pp.05-13.

Pattanaik, Smruti S, "Pakistan's Nuclear Strategy", *Strategic Analysis*, Vol. 27, No. 1, Jan-Mar 2003,pp. 94-115.

Perkovich, George, "Bush's Nuclear Revolution," *Foreign Affairs* Vol.82, no. 2, March-April 2003, pp. 2-8.

Pesaran, M. H, "The System of Dependent Capitalism in Pre- and Post-Revolutionary Iran", *International Journal of Middle East Studies* , Vol.14, no. 4, November 1982, pp. 501-522.

Pollack, Kenneth M, "Iran: Shaking Up the high command," *Policy Watch no. 269,* Washington Institute for Near East Policy, October I, 1997.

Precht, Henry, "The Iranian Revolution 25 Years Later: An Oral History with Henry Precht, Then State Department Desk Officer", *The Middle East Journal*, Vol.58, no. I Winter 2004, pp. 9-31.

Pryor, Leslie M, "Arms and the Shah", *Foreign Policy*, Vol. 31, Summer 1978, pp. 56-71.

Qasim Zaman, Muhammad, "Sectarianism in Pakistan: The radicalization of Shiia and Sunni identities", *Modern Asian studies*, vol.32, 1998, pp.687-716.

Qureshi, Khalida, Pakistan and Iran-A study in neighbourly Diplomacy, Pakistan horizon, Karachi, vol. 21, No.1, First Quarter, 1968, pp. 35-43.

Raman, B, "Iran: An Osirak in the Offing," Paper No. 700, *South Asia Analysis Group,* May 29, 2003.

Ramazani, Rouhollah K, "Challenges for US Policy," in R. K. Rarnazani (ed.), *Iran's Revolution: The Search for Consensus*, Bloomington, Ind.: Indiana University Press, 1990, pp. 125-140.

Ramazani, Rouhollah K. "Iran's Foreign Policy: Condending Orientations", in R. K. Rarnazani (ed.), *Iran's Revolution: The Search for Consensus*, Bloomington, Ind.: Indiana University Press, 1990, pp. 48-68.

Rezun, Miron, "Iran and Afghanistan: With Specific Reference to their Asian Policies and Practices", *Journal of Asian and African Studies*, Vol.25, Nos. 1-2, 1990, p.23.

Rice, Condoleezza.,"Campaign 2000: Promoting the National Interest," *Foreign Affairs* 79, no. (January-February 2000).

Rlchards, Helmut, "America's Shah, Shahanshah's Iran," *MERIP Reports 40* ,September 1975,pp. 3-26.

Ritcheson, Philip L., "Iranian Military Resurgence: Scope, Motivations and Implications for Regional Security", *Armed Forces and Society*, Summer 1995, (21), p.4;

Rottman, Gordon L, "Saddam's Juggernaut or Armed Horde? The Origins of the Iraqi Army", *International Defense Review*, November 1990, pp. 1240-1242.

Roy, Olivier, "The Crisis of Religious Legitimacy in Iran", *The Middle East Journal*, Vol.53, no. 2, Spring 1999, pp.201-217.

Rubin, Barry, "The United States and the Middle East," in Bruce Maddy-Weitzman (ed.), *Middle East Contemporary Survey*, Boulder, Colo.: Westview, 1995, pp. 27-39.

Samii. A, William, "Iran's Guardian Council as an Obstacle to Democracy", *The Middle East Journal* Vol. 55. No. 4, Autumn 2001, 643-662.

Sariolghalam, Mahmood, "Understanding Iran", *The Washington Quarterly*, Autumn 2003, pp., 69-82.

Saunders, Harold H, "The Crisis Begins." in Warren Christopher and Paul H. Kreisberg (ed.), *American Hostages in Iran: The Conduct of a Crisis.* New Haven. Conn.: Yale University Press, 1985, pp.35-71.

Savory, Roger M, "Social Development in Pahlavi Era", George Lenczowski (ed.), *Iran Under the Pahlavis,* Stanford, California: Hoover Institution Press. 1978. pp. 85-127.

Segal. David. "The Iran-Iraq War: A Military Analysis", *Foreign Affairs*, Summer 1988.

Singh, Anoop, "Economics of Iran-Pakistan-India natural gas pipeline", *Economic and Political Weekly*, Vol.43, No.37, 13-19 September 2008, pp.57-65.

Singh, K.R, "A new Axis: China, Pakistan, Afghanistan and Iran", *Defence Watch*, Vol.44, no.4, December 2010, pp14-18.

Singh, S.K., "Evolving Pakistan-Iran Relations", *USI Journal*, Vol. 131, No.545, July-September 2001, pp. 322-33.

Snyder, Robert. "Explaining the Iranian Revolution's Hostility Toward the United States", *Journal of South Asian and Middle Eastern Studies* Vol.17, no. 3 (Spring 1994).

Stein, Janice Gross, "The Wrong Strategy in the Right Place: The United States in the Gulf", *International Security* Vol.13. no. 3 (Winter 1988-1989).

Stobaugh. Robert B. "The Evolution of Iranian Oil Policy, 1925-1975", in George Lenczowski (ed.), *Iran Under the Pahlavis*, Stanford, Calif.: Hoover Institution Press. 1978, pp. 201-252.

Sultan, Razia and Sadia Aziz, "Pakistan and General Zia's Afghan Policy", *South Asian Journal,* Vol.-26, October-December 2009, pp.70-87.

Tahiri, Amir , "Policies of Iran in the Persian gulf Region", in Abbas Ameri (ed.), *The Persian Gulf and the Indian Ocean in International Politics,* Tehran: IPIS, 1975, PP.595-596.

Tahir-Kheli, Shirin, "Iran and Pakistan: Co-Operation in an area of Conflict", Asian Survey, Berkeley, vol.17, no.5, May 1977.

Takeyh, Ray, "God's Will: Iranian Democracy and the Islamic Context", *Middle East Policy 7,* no. 4 (October 2000): 41-49.

Takeyh, Ray, "Iran at Crossroads", *Middle East Journal,* Vol.57, No.1, Winter 2003, pp.42-56.

Taylor, David, "The Politics of Islam and Islamisation in Pakistan, in James Piscatori (ed.), *Islam in the Political process,* Cambridge: Cambridge university Press, 1983.

Terhalle, Maximillan, "Revolutionary Power and Socialization: Explaining the Persistence of Revolutionary Zeal in Iran's Foreign policy", *Security Studies,* Vol.18, 2009, pp.557-586.

Wells, Matthew C, "Thermidor in the Islamic Republic of Iran: The Rise of Muhanunad Khatami", *British Journal of Middle Eastern Studies* 26, no. I, May 1999, pp. 27-39.

Zairing, Lawrence,"From Islamic Republic to Islamic State in Pakistan", *Asian Survey,* Vol-24, no.9, September 1984, pp.933-46.

Zehra, Nasim ,"Pakistan-Iran Relations: Compulsions and Conditions for a Strategic Relationship", *Strategic Studies,* Vol. 23, no.1, spring 2003, pp. 76-89.

Zuberi, Matin, "Pakistan: Epicentre of Nuclear Proliferation", *Journal of Indian Ocean Studies,* Vol.12, No.1, April 2004, pp.01-15.

Zweiri, Mahjoob and Simon Stagffell, "Talking with a Region: Lessons from Iran, Turkey and Pakistan", *Middle East Policy,* Vol. XVI, No.1, 2009, pp.63-74.

ARTICLES IN NEWSPAPERS AND WEBSITES

Abedin, Mahan ,"How to Defeat Jundallah and Its Ilk", *http:// mrzine.monthlyreview.org/2009/abedin231009.html, 23-10-2009*

Adelkhah, Nima, "Iranian Naval Exercises Display Advancements in IRGC Armed Capabilities", April 29, 2010, available at *http:// www.iranembassy.pk/en/political-section/106-perspective-between.html, accessed on 30 September 2010.*

Ahrari, Ehsan, "Pakistan as Proliferator: A View from Washington", Asia Times Online. January 14, 2003 at *http://www.atimes.com/atimes/ South_Asia/EA14Df03.html*

Aneja, Atul,"Warship raises US-Iranian Tensions", *The Hindu*, February 22, 2007.

Aramesh, Arash, "Iran Begins New Round of Naval Exercises in Strait of Hormuz",May 5th, 2010, *http://www.insideiran.org/media-analysis/ iran-begins-new-round-of-naval-exercises-in-strait-of-hormuz*

"Attack in Iran: What are the links to Pakistan?", October 18, 2009, *EDThttp://blogs.reuters.com/pakistan/2009/10/18/attack-in-iran-what-are-the-links-to-pakistan, ACCESSED ON 18 October 2010.*

Barr, Cameron W, "In Iran, Hopes Rise Among the Reformers," *The Christian Science Monitor,* June 11.2001.

Bhadrakumar, M., "What Iran did for India and why it is hurt", *http:// www.rediff.com/news/2005/oct/03spec1.htm*

Bodonsky, Youssef, "Pakistan's Islamic Bomb", July 1998, available at *www.freeman.org*

Boustany, Nora, "The Hostage Labyrinth-Many Complex Deals Lie Behind Any Release." *The Washington Post*, March 18, 2004.

Broder, John M, "Despite a Secret Pact by Gore in '95, Russian Arms Sales to Iran Go On", *The New York Times*, October 13, 2000, p. Al.

Burns, John F, "Top Leader in Iran Tries to Calm Rage of Its Hard-Liners", *The New York Times*. October 2, 1999.

Buzbee, Sally, "A Warning for Iran: Bush Says Don't Help Al-Qaida, Don't Interfere in Afghanistan." *Associated Press*, January 10, 2002.

Charbonneau, Louis, "Iran to Accept Tougher Nuke Checks." *Reuters,* November 8, 2003.

Crossette, Barbara, "Albright, in Overture to Iran, Seeks a 'Road Map' to Amity." *The New York Times,* June 18, 1998.

Daniszewski, John, "Landslide Election in Iran; A Mullah with Open Mind, Khatami Won by Dint of Character." *Los Angeles Times*, May 25, 1997, p. AIO.

Douglas Frantz, "Iran closes in on Ability to build a nuclear bomb", *The Los Angeles Times*, August 4, 2003.

Efron, Sonni and Douglas Frantz, "Secret Iran Nuclear Plan Discovered", *The Los Angeles Times*, February 13, 2004.

Ellison, Katherine, "Argentina, Iran on Verge of Severing Diplomatic Relations." Knight *Ridders Tribune News Service*, May 20. 1998.

Erlanger, Steven, "Iran Vote May Bring Pressure for a Change in U.S. Policy." *The New York Times,* May 26,1997.

Faramarzi, Scheherezade, "Khomeini Contains Dissent over Arms Deal with Washington." *Associated Press*, December 6, 1986.

Farley, Maggie and Bob Dogrin, "Evil behind the Axis", *The Los Angeles Times*, January 5, 2003.

Faruqi, Anwar, "Thousands Rally for Iranian Candidate in Test for Ruling Clergy." *Associated Press*, May 21,1997.

Gannon, Kathy. "US. Fears Iranian Interference in Afghanistan; Aid Agencies Fan Out to Starving Afghans." *Associated Press,* January 18, 2002.

Ghoddoosi, Pooneh, "Postcards from Iran: Tehran Party." *BBC News*, February 13, 2004. Available at *news.bbc.co.uk/go/pr/fr/-/l/hi/world/ middle3ast/3486779.stm, accessed May 24, 2004.*

Goodenough, Patrick, "Iran, Pakistan Push Ahead With Gas Pipeline Deal", *CNSNEWS.COM*, June 14, 2010, available on *http://www.cnsnews.com/ news/article/67654*

Gordon, Michael R and Eric Schmitt, "Iran Nearly Got a Missile Alloy from Russians." *The New York Times*. April 25, 1998, p. AI.

Hanley, Charles, "American Detention of Iranian General, Others May Set Off Violence, Afghan Says." *Associated Press*, March 9, 2002.

Hasnat, S.F.,"Stagnating Pakistan-Iran Relations", December 01, 2006, available at 2006, *http://www.chowk.com/articles/11418, accessed on 16 August 2010.*

Hersh, Seymour M, "The Iran Game: How Will Tehran's Nuclear Ambitions Affect Our Budding Partnership?" *The New Yorker*, December 3, 2001, p. 42.

Hirst, David, "Iran Warns Gulf States over Oil." *The Guardian*, August 23 1986, p. 1.

"IPI Pipeline Moves Ahead, Defying U.S " *http://www.india-server.com/news/ipi-pipeline-moves-ahead-defying-u-s—3777.html, accessed on 01 December 2010*

"Iranian commanders assassinated", *http://news.bbc.co.uk/2/hi/8312964.stm*

"Iran, Pakistan Sign 4 MoUs on Mutual Cooperation," *Fars News Agency*, June 30, 2008.

"Iran, Pakistan to Enhance Trade Volume by $1 Bn.," *Fars News Agency*, June 27, 2008.

"Iran's supreme leader backs Kashmir 'struggle", *Indo-Asian News Service*, Tehran, November 19, 2010 available at *http://www.hindustantimes.com/Iran-s-supreme-leader-backs-Kashmir-struggle/Article1-628346.aspx, accessed on 22 November 2010*

"Iran vows revenge after blast kills six Revolutionary Guards commanders and 37 others in Sistan-Baluchistan province", 18 October 2009, *http://www.guardian.co.uk/world/2009/oct/18/iran-suicide-bomb-revenge-vow*

Iqwal, Anwar, "Father of Pakistan's Bomb in Trouble", *The Washington Times*, January 8, 2003.

Jehl, Douglas, "Iran Closes a Leading Newspaper and Arrests Top Editors." *The New York Times,* September 18, 1998.

Johns, Richard and Lucy Kellaway, "Iraq Hits Hormuz Strait Oil Terminal." *Financial Times,* November 26, 1986, p. 1.

Johnson, Haynes, "Hostages to the Past." *The Washington Post.* July 9,1991.

"Jundallah: Iran's Sunni rebels", 20 Jun 2010, *11:25http://english.aljazeera.net/news/middleeast/2010/06/201062074140996374.html,accessed 0n 18 October 2010.*

Kelley, Matt, "Iran Has Allowed Taliban, al-Quida Members to Escape, Rumsfeld Says." *Associated Press*, February 3, 2002.

Kerr, Paul, "IAEA Presses to Iran to comply with Nuclear Safeguards", *Arms Control Today,* July/August 2003, pp.20-22.

Kinzer, Stephen, "Moderate Leader Is Elected in Iran by a Wide Margin." *The New York Times,* May 25,1997.

Kruthammer, Charles, "Axis of Evil, Part Two", *The Washington Post*, July 23, 2004, p. A 29.

Lake, Eli, "US Iran Had Talks on Prisoner Deal", *The New York Sun*, December 15, 2003.

Landler, Mark, "Iran Threatens to Restart Nuclear Work", *The New York Times,* June 17,2004, p. A10.

Levi, Michael, "Nuclear Reaction: Why Won't the IAEA Get Tough with Iran?" *The New Republic*, September 5, 2003.

Lewis, Paul, "War on Oil Tankers Heats up in the Persian Gulf." *The New York Times,* May 18, 1986, p. 1.

Lotfi, Rozita, "Iranian Postcards: Wrapped in Red Tape." *BBC News*, February 13, 2004. *Available at news.bbc.co.uklgo/pr/fr/-/l/hi/worldlmiddle_east/3487249.stm, accessed May 24, 2004.*

MacFarquhar, Neil, "Backlash of Intolerance Stirring Fear in Iran." *The New York Times,* September 20, 1996.

MacLeod, Scott, "Radicals Reborn: Iran's Student Heroes Have Had a Rough and Surprising Passage." *Time*, November 15, 1999.

Maddox, Browen, "Iran admits Pakistan gave Key Nuclear Help", *The London Times,* November 13, 2003

Maleki, Abbas, "Iran's Regional Foreign/Energy Policy", *www.caspianstudies.com, accessed on 03 April 2010.*

Milhollin, Gary, "The Mullahs and the Bomb." *The New York Times,* October 23, 2003.

Mitchell, Alison, "Clinton Sees Hope in the Election of Moderate as President of Iran." *The New York Times*, May 30,1997.

Montazeran, Ahmed and Mumtaz, Kashif, "Iran-Pakistan: Cooperation For Regional Stability And Peace", available at *http://www.issi.org.pk/ journal/2004_files/no_1/article/3a.htm*

Mufson, Steven, "Chinese Nuclear Officials See No Reason to Change Plans to Sell Reactor to Iran." *The Washington Post*, May 18, 1995, p. A22.

Muhammad, Z. G,"Trouble in Kashmir's paradise", September 26, 2010 *http://www.tehrantimes.com/index_View.asp?code=227357,tehran times, October 5, 2010*

Muir, Jim, "Iran to Review Academic's Verdict." BBC News, November 25, 2002. Available at *news.bbc.co.ukllllow/worldimiddlc38St/ 2511941.stm, uccessed August 5, 2004.*

Omer, K, "Gwador: An emerging gateway to Central Asia", *The News*, 22 April 2007, p.111.

"Pakistan's Khan sold Iran Nuclear Parts, Police say", Reuters, February 20, 2004;

"Pakistan not intimidated by US on pipeline", 14 June 2005, *http:// forum.pakistanidefence.com/lofiversion/index.php/t45891.html, accessed on 01 December 2010.*

"Pakistan PM Seeks Wider Trade with Iran, Turkey," *Indo-Asian News Service*, November 11, 2007.

"Pakistan to Import 1,000 MW of Electricity from Iran," *Fars News Agency*, August 11, 2008.

"Pakistan's foreign economic relations", available at *http:// countrystudies.us/pakistan/47.htm accessed on 16 august 2010.*

"Perspective of Ties between the I.R.Iran and Pakistan" *http:// www.iranembassy.pk/en/political-section/106-perspective- between.html, accessed on 30 September 2010.*

Pan, Esther and Sharon Otterman. "Iran: Curtailing the Nuclear Program." The Council on Foreign Relations, May 13. 2004, available at *www.cfr.org/background/iran_curtail.php?print=accessed May 14, 2004.*

Perlmutter, Amos, "Tracing the Terror Trail Back to Iran," *The Washington Times*, June 23, 1997, 1 p.A13.

Ranjan, Amitav, "Iran Pipeline: Now runs into US Sanctions", *The Indian Express*, 28 May 2003.

Rohan Sullivan, "Sources give details of Iran Nuke Deal", *The Washington Times*, February 20, 2004.

Samanta, Pranab Dhal, "Iran-slams-India-over-jandk-protests-india-hits-back", *Indian express,* 5 October 2010.

Sanger, David E, "In Face of Report: Iran Acknowledges Buying Nuclear Components." *The New York Times*. February 23, 2004.

Schmemann, Serge, "Giving War a Chance." *The New York Times*. April 14. 1996.

Schweid, Barry, "U.S. to Punish Chinese for Chemical Weapons Shipments to Iran." *Associated Press*. May 22 1997.

Sciolino, Elaine, "Beijing Rebuffs U.S. on Halting Iran Atom Dea!." *The New York Times*. Apti118; 1995. p. A1.

Scowcroft, Brent, "An Opening to Iran." *The Washington Post*. May 11. 2001.

"Shah Reviews Foreign Policy", *Asian Recorder*, vol.12, no.33, 13-19 August 1966, p.7235.

"Suicide attack targeting Iran troops: President Mahmoud Ahmadinejad promises sharp retaliation", *http://www.msnbc.msn.com/id/33366170/*

Sipress, Alan, "Bush's Speech Shuts Door on Tenuous Opening to Iran." *The Washington Post,* February 4. 2002. p. AIO.

Slackman, Michael ,"Iran Blames U.S. and Britain in Attack", October 19, 2009; *http://www.nytimes.com/2009/10/20/world/middleeast/20iran.html*

Slavin, Bartara, "Iran, U.S. Holding Talks in Geneva." *USA Today*, May 11,2003.

Smith, R. Jeffrey, "China May Cancel Proposed Sale of Nuclear Facility to Iran." *The Washington Post,* November 6, 1996. p. A9.

Smith, Stefan, "Iran Admits Resuming Centrifuge Assembly; European Powers Report 'No Progress' in Talks." *Agence France-Presse*. August 6. 2004.

Sokolski, Henry, "That Iranian Nuclear Headache," National Review Online, January 22.2004. Available at *www.npec-web.org, accessed January 22. 2004.*

Squassoni, Sharon, "Iran's Nuclear Program: Recent Developments"; CRS Report for Congress, Order Code RS21592, Updated November 12, 2003, p.crs-1, *available at http://www.parstimes.com/nuclear/ crs_nov03.pdf, accessed on April 10, 2010.*

Stockman, Farah, "Unease Builds with Rise of Iran." *The Boston Globe.* August 4, 2004, p. AI.

Sullivan, Rohan, "Sources give details of Iran Nuke Deal", *The Washington Times,* February 20, 2004.

Summary of World Broadcasts (SWB), BBC, December 10, 1999, Third Series ME/3714.

Tehran Times, 30 May 2010,

Tyler, Patrick E, "Russian's Links to Iran Offer a Case Study in Arms Leaks." *The New York Times,* May 10, 2000, p. A6 .

Valinejad, Afshin. "Iran Denies Giving Refuge to al-Qaida or Taliban, Admits It Can't Fully Control Borders." *Associated Press*, February 5, 2002.

Varadarajan, Siddharth, "Iran and the invention of a nuclear crisis", The Hindu, Sep 21, 2005, http://www.hinduonnet.com/2005/09/21/stories/ 2005092105231000.htm

Vick, Karl, "Another Nuclear Program Found in Iran." *The Washing/on Post*, February 24, 2004, p. A I.

Waldman, Amy, "After Mixup, Americans Free 12 Afghans Suspected of Being Iranian Agents", *The New York Times*, March 2 I, 2002.

Wallace, Charles P, "Khomeini Blasts Aides for Secret Talks with U.S." *Los Angeles Times,* November   21,1986, p. 1.

Warrick, Joby,"Nuclear Program in Iran Tied to Pakistan", The Washington Post, December 21, 2003, p.A01;

Warrick, Joby and Glenn Kessler. "Iran Had Secret Nuclear Program, UN Agency Says." *The Washing/on Post,* November 11,2003, p. AI.

Weiner, Tim, "U.S. Plan to Change Iran Leaders Is an Open Secret Before It Begins." *The New York Times*, January 26, 1996, p. 1.

Weiss, Leonard and Larry Diamond, "Congress must stop an attack on Iran", *The Los Angeles Times*, February 5, 2007

Weymouth, Lally, "It's Peace or a New Wave of Terrorism, Says Rabin." *The Washington Post,* June 21, 1995, p. A21.

Wright, Robin, "In Shift, U.S. Makes Quiet Overtures to Iran Following Election Upset." *Los Angeles , Times*, July 9,1997. .

Yusufzai, Rahimullah, "Pakistan-Afghan Relations: Hostage to the Past", *http://www.Cacianalyst.Org.*

"Zardari, Karzai, Ahmadinejad hold trilateral meeting", 11 March 2009, *http://www.onepakistan.com/news/national/6454-iran-zardari-karzai-ahmadinejad-hold-trilateral-meeting.*

Zubairy, Sahar, "Iran Mourns", October 21st 2009, *http://iran.foreignpolicyblogs.com/tag/irgc/*

APPENDIX-I

SAAD-ABAD PACT OR TREATY:

[1]Traduction-Translation

No. 4402-Treaty[2] of Non-Aggression between the Kingdom of Afghanistan, The Kingdom of Iraq, the Empire of Iran and the Republic of Turkey, Signed at Teheran, July 8th, 1937.

————————————————————————————

(League of Nations — Treaty Series, the Registration of this treaty took place July 19th 1938)

————————————————————————————

PREAMBLE.

HIS IMPERIAL MAJESTY THE SHAHINSHAH OF IRAN,

HIS MAJESTY THE KING OF AFGHANISTAN,

HIS MAJESTY THE KING OF IRAQ,

THE PRESIDENT OF THE REPUBLIC OF TURKEY;

Being desirous of contributing by every means in their power to the maintenance of friendly and harmonious relations between them;

Actuated by the common purpose of ensuring peace and security in the Near East by means of additional guarantees within the framework of the Covenant of the League of Nations, and of thus contributing to general peace ; and

Deeply conscious of their obligations under the Treaty[3] for Renunciation of War, signed at Paris on August 27th, 1928, and of the other treaties to which they are parties, all of which are in harmony with the Covenant of the League of Nations and the Treaty for Renunciation of War;

Have decided to conclude the present Treaty and have for that purpose appointed:

HIS IMPERIAL MAJESTY THE SHAHINSHAH OF IRAN:

> His Excellency Monsieur Enayatollah SAMIY, Minister for Foreign Affairs of Iran;

HIS MAJESTY THE KING OF AFGHANISTAN:

> His Excellency Monsieur FAIZ MOHAMMAD Khan, Minister for Foreign Affairs of Afghanistan;

HIS MAJESTY THE KING OF IRAQ:

> His Excellency Dr. NADJI-AL-ASIL, Minister for Foreign Affairs of Iraq;

THE PRESIDENT OF THE REPUBLIC OF TURKEY:

> His Excellency Dr. Tevfik RUSTU ARAS, Minister for Foreign Affairs of Turkey;

Who, having exchanged their full powers, found in good and due form, have agreed upon the following provisions:

Article 1.

The High Contracting Parties undertake to pursue a policy of complete abstention from any interference in each other's internal affairs.

Article 2.

The High Contracting Parties expressly undertake to respect the inviolability of their common frontiers.

Article 3.

The High Contracting Parties agree to consult together in all international disputes affecting their common interests.

Article 4.

Each of the High Contracting Parties undertakes in no event to resort, whether singly or jointly with one or more third Powers, to any act of aggression directed against any other of the Contracting Parties.

The following shall be deemed to be acts of aggression:

1. Declaration of war;

2. Invasion by the armed forces of one State, with or without a declaration of war, of the territory of another State ;

3. An attack by the land, naval or air forces of one State, with or without a declaration of war, on the territory, vessels or aircraft of another State;

4. Directly or indirectly aiding or assisting an aggressor.

The following shall not constitute acts of aggression:

1. The exercise of the right of legitimate self-defence, that is to say, resistance to an act   of aggression as defined above ;

2. Action under Article 16 of the Covenant of the League of Nations;

3. Action in pursuance of a decision of the Assembly or Council of the League of Nations, or under Article 15, paragraph 7, of the Covenant of the League of Nations, provided always that in the latter case such action is directed against the State which was the first to attack ;

4. Action to assist a State subjected to attack, invasion or recourse to war by another of the High Contracting Parties, in violation of the Treaty for Renunciation of War signed in Paris on August 27th, 1928.

Article 5.

Should one of the High Contracting Parties consider that a breach of Article 4 of the present Treaty has been or is about to be committed, he shall at once bring the matter before the Council of the League of Nations.

The foregoing provision shall not affect the right of such High Contracting Party to take any steps which, in the circumstances, he may deem necessary.

Article 6.

Should one of the High Contracting Parties commit an aggression against a third Power, any other High Contracting Party may denounce the present Treaty, without notice, as towards the aggressor.

Article 7.

Each of the High Contracting Parties undertakes to prevent, within his respective frontiers, the formation or activities of armed bands, associations or organisations to subvert the established institutions, or disturb the order or security of any part, whether situated on the frontier or elsewhere, of the territory of another Party, or to change the constitutional system of such other Party.

Article 8.

The High Contracting Parties, having already recognised, in the General Treaty for Renunciation of War of August 27th, 1928, that the settlement or solution of all disputes or conflicts, whatever their nature or origin, which may arise among them, shall never be sought by other than pacific means, reaffirm that principle and undertake to rely upon such modes of procedure as have been or shall be established between the High Contracting Parties in that respect.

Article 9.

No Articles of the present Treaty shall be considered as in any waydiminishing the obligations assumed by each of the High Contracting Parties under the Covenant of the League of Nations.

Article 10.

The present Treaty, drawn up in the French language and signed in quadruplicate, one copy having, as they severally recognise, been delivered to each of the High Contracting Parties, is concluded for a period of five years.

On the expiry of that period, and failing its denunciation, with six months' notice, by one of the High Contracting Parties, the Treaty shall be deemed to be renewed for successive periods of five years, until its denunciation with six months' notice by one or more of the High Contracting Parties. On its denunciation as towards one of the Parties, the Treaty shall nevertheless remain in force as between the others.

The present Treaty shall be ratified by each of the High Contracting Parties in accordance with its Constitution, and registered at the League of Nations by the Secretary-General, who shall be requested to bring it to the knowledge of the other Members of the League.

The instruments of ratification shall be deposited by each of the High Contracting Parties with the Iranian Government.

On the deposit of instruments of ratification by two of the High Contracting Parties, the present Treaty shall at once come into force as between those two Parties. It shall come into force as regards the third and fourth Parties respectively on the deposit of their instruments of ratification.

On the deposit of each instrument of ratification, the Government of Iran shall immediately notify all the signatories of the present Treaty.

Done at the Palace of Saad-Abad (Teheran), on the eighth day of July, one thousand nine hundred and thirty-seven.

Enayatollah SAMIY,   FAIZ MOHAMMAD Khan,
Minister for Foreign Affairs   *Minister for Foreign Affairs*
of Iran.   *of Afghanistan.*

Dr. NADJI-AL-ASIL,   Dr. Tevfik RUSTU ARAS,
Minister for Foreign Affairs   *Minister for Foreign Affairs*
of Iraq.   of Turkey.

_____

*Source: UN Treaty, "League of Nations-Treaty Series-1938",
available at untreaty.un.org/unts/60001_120000/19/21/
00037047.pdf*

APPPENDIX-II

ADDRESS BY THE PRIME MINISTER TO THE IRANIAN MAJLIS TEHRAN: NOVEMBER 8,1995

Speaker All Akbar Nateq Nouri,

Excellencies,

I consider it an honour to address the elected representatives of the Islamic Republic of Iran. Iran has a long and ancient history, a rich cultural heritage, a distinctive language. Its history, heritage, language have left their imprints far and wide in our region.

The Islamic Revolution in Iran came about as the result of a long struggle, the sacrifices of many martyrs, the sufferings of many more. It was the popular uprising of a people determined to take charge of their own destiny. The Islamic Revolution was closely followed by the rest of the world and fiercely defended by the people of Iran.

Shortly after its inception, the Revolution, we caught in an unfortunate conflict. The people of Iran once again faced this new challenge with fortitude. We are glad that peace has now dawned and the people of Iran are engaged in the task of nation building under the guidance of their new elected representatives. I mention this history to recall the sense of sacrifice which the people of Iran have demonstrated to defend what they believe in irrespective of the cost.

We in Pakistan too have struggled and sacrificed for what we believed in. The creation of Pakistan itself was the result of the struggle and sacrifices of the Muslims of South Asia, under the leadership of Quaid-e-Azam Mohammed Ali Jinnah. Many of the opponents of Pakistan thought, it would not survive the difficulties caused for it at its inception. But the people of Pakistan rose to the challenge and defended the nation state against all threats. In three wars Pakistan upheld its sovereignty and independence.

Deeply conscious of the needs for Islamic solidarity and of the struggle against colonialism, Pakistan has been in the forefront of all Muslim causes. Whether it was the independence of Algeria or Tunisia or Morocco, it played a critical role. Equally, Pakistan raised its voice for the people of Kashmir, Palestine, Zimbabwe, and Namibia and against apartheid. More recently, Pakistan along with Iran and other countries of the world helped its Afghan brethren to resist the foreign occupation of Afghanistan. We raised our voice for the people of Bosnia-Herzegovina along with the people of Iran and all justice loving people of the world.

Iran and Pakistan are not only two neighbouring but we are two Muslim countries. Islam binds us together in a spiritual bond which others cannot share in the same manner. Islamic principles have helped guide our people and shape our destiny. If Iran and Pakistan have raised their voice for the people of Kashmir, Palestine, Bosnia, Afghanistan it is because Islam binds upon us to speak the truth and uphold the banner of justice or the just cause. Islam makes it incumbent upon its followers to help the weak, the poor, the oppressed, thus it has a human dimension which shapes our thoughts and actions.

All Muslims, wherever we may be greet each other wish the word "As-salaam-o-Alaikum" which means "Peace Be Upon You", Therefore, Iran and Pakistan seek peace wherever we see conflict. All Muslims face the Holy Ka'aba when we bow down to pray. In this act of prayer is the demonstration of our unity.

Some elements would not like to see unity within the Muslim world. Some elements would like to divide the Muslim world on sectarian lines. Such elements are not sincere with Islam and the Muslim world. Muslim peoples and we Muslim countries must beware of such elements. The rise of sectarianism would weaken us, divide us, and undermine our aims, objectives and goals. All Muslims are Muslims whether they belong to one sect or another.

In unity lies our strength and in unity lies our common identity, our hopes for the future and the attainment of our common goals for the prosperity of our people and the dignity of our nation states. With the end of the Cold War, we have witnessed the decline of the Order, which dominated the world since World War-II ended. This was a world of ideological camps, where different groups were identified as left or Right.

Now we see the rise; in some areas, of new dangers, the dangers of ethnicity or tribalism. In Islam there is no place for ethnicity, racial prejudice, tribalism or discrimination. In Islam all human beings are equal before the eyes of Almighty Allah irrespective of their ethnic, tribal or racial affiliations. .In this we see again the message of unity. And because we believe in the convent of unity and repudiate discrimination we seek a World Order which is just and equal. And that is why we oppose tyranny and injustice.

The end of the Cold War has seen the winds of freedom and democracy blow across the world. Iron curtains have been lifted. The Berlin Wall has fallen. We have welcomed the process of greater democratization within nations. However, the process of democratization within nations is not sufficient. We need greater democratization between nation states too.

Recently Iran and Pakistan both participated in the Golden Jubilee of the United Nations. It was a time for reflection. It was time to recollect what we had achieved and what we still needed to achieve. While we have achieved global peace, regional conflicts continue to cast dark shadows on the international horizon. One such major regional conflict which has remained unresolved is the Kashmir dispute. The Secretary General of the United Nations has described this dispute as one of the oldest unresolved items on the agenda of the United Nations.

More than 600,000 occupying troops have failed to crush the indomitable spirit of the Kashmiri people. Dawn to dusk curfews, gang rapes of women, summary trials, arbitrary detention, custodial deaths, and widespread torture are some of the atrocities committed. Acts of sacrilege have been carried out in an attempt to destroy the freedom movement. Such acts have provoked the sensibilities of the Kashmiri people, the Muslim people and all people who oppose sacrilege.

Who can forget siege of the Holy Hazrat Bal shrine in the valley of Kashmir? Who can forget the burning of the Mosque and Mazar at Charar Shareef? Who can forget that this was done by those who burnt the Babri Masjid? Such acts were aimed not only against the Kashmiri people but against all Muslims. These acts cannot be forgotten by anyone anywhere these acts cannot be forgotten or forgiven by the Kashmiri people. They will be passed from generation to generation.

Pakistan and Iran stand shoulder to shoulder in support of the Kashmiri people in their struggle for self determination. We recall the historic words of President Rafsanjani in the Parliament of Pakistan and I quote "Kashmir issue is your problem and it is also our problem too, because it Islamic problem. Like you we complain against the United Nations why do they not enforce and implement their resolutions and why do they allow bloodshed." Iran, Pakistan and the entire Muslim world at the historic Casablanca Conference in a declaration in December 1994 called for the resolution of the Kashmir dispute in accordance with United Nations Resolutions. So-called elections will not satisfy the people of Kashmir who are demanding plebiscite with one voice under the banner of the All Parties Hurriyat Conference.

Pakistan and Iran have condemned Serbian aggression against Bosnia Herzegovina. The naked aggression against Bosnia in the heart of Europe telecast across the world is a stain on the conscience of mankind. The world has shown a dismal failure to put into place security mechanisms to uphold the Charter of United Nations. The world has forgotten that two World Wars sprang in one-way or another from Sarajevo. Recently some moves have been made to bring about a political settlement. We hope that these moves will be to the satisfaction of the people of Bosnia-Herzegovina that will lead to peace. However, the tragedy in Bosnia has made one thing clear: That is that each nation must be prepared to defend itself. If it cannot defend itself, it will be swallowed up and blotted out.

Unless a country has a strategic importance to the rest of the world, the rest of the world will ignore it or be slow in responding to it. The slow response may lead to a fait accompli in itself. We are aware that some of our friends have argued that the world was slow in responding to the ulterior purpose of allowing the aggressors the time to fulfil the aims of their aggression. It we only the spirit of the Bosnian people that thwarted this tragedy:

I must say the Muslim world through the OIC Contact Group on Bosnia also contributed in a humble way to keep the issue alive, to assist and to coordinate global and regional moves along with the Government of Bosnia. But if there is one clear lesson i.e. that each country must be prepared to defend itself if it is not crucial to the larger world. To be critical one has to have access to critical sea passages or energy flows which can adversely affect global trade. Thus nations are judged by their impact on global trade.

One example of a country ravaged by civil war is Afghanistan. The world united when Afghanistan was under foreign occupation to defend not only freedom in Afghanistan but to defend the free world. Now that there is no threat to the free world, Afghanistan is a forgotten global story. Since Afghanistan has no bearing on the flow of global commerce, it has no impact on world opinion. Except for handful of countries, the world has forgotten Afghanistan. Every now and then cursory references are made about Afghanistan. Just references. Very little substantive action. Both the United Nations and OIC have sent representatives to the Kabul regime but the Kabul regime has been fending them off to gain time.

My heart bleeds for the brave people of Afghanistan. A whole generation of young people have grown up in war, known only conflict, seen only sufferings. They live against the background music of mortar and rockets. They live amongst the ravaged land with poverty, hunger and insecurity. Peace is the message of Islam. But the leaders and commanders seem to have substituted the message of peace for the message of power. They fight each other for power. This is most unfortunate. We in Pakistan have decided not to give materkl or military assistance to any faction.

We believe that the term of the Kabul regime is over. We condemn the Kabul regime for burning our Embassy in a premeditated attack. We note the Kabul regime has fallen into the arms of those who seek to destroy the people and yet we do not interfere. When President Rafsanjani addressed the Parliament of Pakistan, he said: "In fact no one but a mad man who wants to kill himself would like to interfere in Afghanistan in such a severe situation". Today the sister of President Rafsanjani is here to repeat his words as our own sentiments in the Parliament of Iran.

Mr. Speaker,

We continue to give refuge to 1.5 million refugees from Afghanistan because the despicable acts against us by the Kabul regime do not reflect the wishes of the vast majority of the Afghan people. We do so because it is our policy not to interfere in Afghanistan; we want the dust to settle down. We want natural leaders to emerge. We want the Afghans to solve their problems themselves, of course we keep our channel of communications open with all groups and we shall continue to do so. We keep our country open for all groups. All Afghan group leaders are welcome to visit Pakistan. Both Iran and Pakistan indeed are geographical neighbours of Afghanistan. We are concerned about the instability in Afghanistan and will continue to watch over the situation closely. We in Pakistan believe the UN and OIC should redouble their efforts for a political solution. We do not believe any one group in Afghanistan has the strength or influence to rule over all Afghanistan. Different groups will need to come together and decide on a formula of power sharing. Such an event will help expedite a political solution. Pakistan's foreign policy is based on principles. We are good friends. Our history shows that we do not change friends with changing season. We believe in keeping friends and nurturing friendships. Our relations with one country are never at the cost of our relations with another country.

When America and China were not on speaking terms, we had relations with both. Their disagreements were their disagreements. If we did anything, it was to counsel both to come closer and bridge the differences. We consider Iran a friend; a neighbour, a brother in Islam. I recall the words of President Rafsanjani when he said to the Pakistani Parliament: "It is a cruel allegation against us that we both are rivals and are competing against each other. Rivalry for what? There is no rivalry between us— And if anyone thinks that Iran and Pakistan are having their own interests in interfering in Afghanistan, then no doubt, he is crazy?" A segment of public opinion has started such rumours which are baseless.

Those who are jealous of the friendship between Iran and Pakistan, those who would like to see the security of Iran and Pakistan weakened, those who would like to create differences between two leading members of the Muslim Ummah, perhaps they would like to see Iran and Pakistan as rivals. They would like to see Iran and Pakistan competing against each other. Neither the leadership, the governments, the people not the elected representatives of Iran and Pakistan can dream of the day when we would be rivals or compete with each other. We are friends. Friends because of principles, friends because of geography, friends because of religion. Friends because we trust each other and need each other and because our mutual security and well being rests on this trust and this friendship. If anyone seeks to undermine the security of Iran, the Iranian Nation knows it can rely on Pakistan. And if anyone tries to undermine the security of Pakistan, the Pakistani Nation knows it can rely on Iran.

Mr. Speaker,

While markets are taking the place of missiles as a measure of might, we cannot turn a blind eye to those who seek to dominate with military might. In our region, one country is building up a mighty military arsenal. It is determined to build blue water navy. It has started production of short range missiles which can be deployed in half an hour. These missiles can target every single city in Pakistan. These missiles are capable of carrying nuclear warheads. After this, this country intends to develop more missiles with a greater range. This country seeks to develop missiles capable of carrying nuclear warheads all the way from Yemen to the straits of Mallaca. This country, which is a non-Muslim country, seeks to bring mostly Muslim countries from Yemen to straits of Mallaca under the cover of its range. We believe that if this country did not have far-reaching ambitions, it would not seek to make missiles of such range and carrying such lethal weapons.

The development of such missiles will cast the shadow of nuclear threat to the sovereignty of Iran, Iraq, Syria, Kuwait, and Saudi Arabia to the West and to Malaysia, Singapore, Indonesia and Brunie to the East. Pakistan deplores this missile build-up which threatens to start a broader missile race. Pakistan calls for a regional solution to the missile issue.

Pakistan does not wish to see nuclear proliferation or the spread of the weapons of mass destruction. Pakistan cautions the world to awaken to the danger boiling in the cauldron before it overflows with dangerous consequences for regional and international peace and stability.

Mr. Speaker Sir,

As a Muslim woman, it gladdens my heart to see my Iranian sisters take their place with pride in the Iranian Parliament. In August, Pakistan hosted a Conference of Women Parliamentarians from Muslim Countries. More than one hundred women representatives from 35 Muslim countries participated in the Conference. The large participation by our Muslim sisters showed that a great awakening is taking place amongst the Muslim women. This awareness amongst Muslim women first took price at the dawn of Islam. No one can forget that God chose a woman, Hazrat Bibi Khadija, to be the first witness to Islam. No one can forget that the Holy Prophet (Peace Be Upon Him) married a working woman. No one can forget that God chose a woman, Hazrat Bibi Fatima, through whom the line of the Holy Prophet (PBUH) was passed on through the generations.

How can we forget that Bibi Fatima is the daughter of the Holy Prophet (PBUH), the daughter of the first convert to Islam, the wife of Hazrat Ali. the mother of the Imams. That God chose one woman for so many exalted positions has a meaning which we need to appreciate. Women in Islam must be accorded respect, dignity and rights bequeathed by Allah in the Holy Book as recited by the Holy Prophet (PBUH).

Mr. Speaker,

I thank you once again on my own behalf and the behalf of the Pakistani people for inviting me to address the Iranian Nation through its Parliament and elected representatives. This is a singular honour that I am the first female chief executive who has been accorded this honour and the first Pakistani chief executive.

Mr. Speaker,

You can count on our friendship. We shall continue to cooperate in the years ahead as we have in the past.

Thank you very much.

Source: *Foreign Affairs Pakistan,* November-December 1995, pp. 12-20.

APPENDIX-III

JOINT PRESS STATEMENT ISSUED ON THE CONCLUSION OF THE VISIT OF H.E. MOHTARMA BENAZIR BHUTTO, PRIME MINISTER OF THE ISLAMIC REPUBLIC OF PAKISTAN TO THE ISLAMIC REPUBLIC OF IRAN, 6-8 NOVEMBER 1995

1.   At the invitation of H.E. Hojjat-ul-Islam-val-Moslemin Akbar Hashemi Rafsanjani, President of the Islamic Republic of Iran, H.E. Mohtarma Benazir Bhutto, Prime Minister of the Islamic Republic of Pakistan paid an official visit to the Islamic Republic of Iran from 6th to 8th November, 1995.

2.   The Prime Minister of the Islamic Republic of Pakistan was accompanied by a high level delegation comprising Ministers, Parliamentarians and senior officials. During their stay in Iran, Prime Minister Mohtarma Benazir Bhutto and her entourage were accorded a warm cordial welcome, characteristic of the close brotherly relations existing between the two fraternal countries.

3.   The Prime Minster of Pakistan and her accompanying entourage visited the holy city of Mashhad and paid homage at the shrine of Hazrat Imam Reza (A.S). They also visited the mausoleum of the Leader of Islamic Revolution and the Founder of the Islamic Republic of Iran, Imam Khomeini, to pay their respects.

4.   During her visit Prime Minister Mohtarma Benazir Bhutto met with the Speaker of the Islamic Consultative Assembly (Majlis) H.E Ali Akbar Nategh Nouri and exchanged views with him on matters of mutual interest. Prime Minister was also accorded the unique honour of addressing the Islamic Consultative Assembly.

5.   The President and the Prime Minister underscored the historical and religious bonds between the two countries which served as a foundation for the further strengthening and expansion of bilateral as well as multilateral cooperation.

6.   They exchanged views on the entire spectrum of bilateral relations. They also   discussed regional   developments   and international issues   of common concern.   The discussions were held in a warm and friendly atmosphere, marked by complete understanding and commonality of views.

7.   The two sides noted with satisfaction the increase in bilateral trade volume during 1994-95 and stressed the need for further consolidation of this positive trend. In the field of economic cooperation, they expressed their appreciation for the speed with which the major bilateral economic projects such as the oil refinery and gas pipeline were moving forward. They also noted the progress made on the bulldozers, sugar, cement paints deal and felt that their early finalization would give major boost to industrial collaboration between the two countries.

Both sides stressed the need for promotion of cooperation between the private sectors, especially the chambers of commerce and industries of the two countries.

8.   During the visit the following documents were signed:

- Agreement on Reciprocal Promotion and Protection of Investments.

- Agreement on the Maritime Commercial Navigation.

- Agreement on the Establishment of Joint Business Council (JBC).

- M.O.U. for Cooperation in the field of Women Sports.

- M.O.U. for the review of the implementation of the Joint Economic Commission.

9.   Both sides welcomed an increase in the exchange of delegations at the level of Heads of States/Governments, officials as

well as experts between the two countries with a view to further deepen the bilateral relations.

10.   The President and the Prime Minister reiterated their resolve to eliminate the trafficking and smuggling of narcotics across the Pak-Iran border and towards this end, agreed to intensify cooperation and devise effective measures. They also decided that during the forthcoming visit of the interior minister of Iran to Pakistan, these issues should be considered as is other matters of mutual interest.

11.   The two sides reaffirmed their commitment to the goals and objectives of ECO. They recalled with satisfaction the outcome of the historic ECO Summit, held in Islamabad in March 1995, leading to the signing agreements for the establishment of several ECO institutions. Noting the importance of these institutions for ECO to function as an effective instrument of regional cooperation, they stressed the need for their early establishment. In this context, they underlined the need for the member states to complete the ratification procedures as soon as possible. They issued the hope that this process would be completed before the Fourth ECO Summit to be held in Asghabad in April 1996.

12.   Both sides stressed the importance of bilateral cooperation in bolstering mutually beneficial trade and economic links with Central Asian as well as the expansion of regional economic cooperation as a major element not contributing to regional peace and stability.

13.   The regional situation constituted a major topic in the talks of the two sides. They stressed the importance of preservation of peace and tranquillity in the Indian Ocean as well as the Persian Gulf by the states. Both sides noted that all major problems and differences in the region must be peacefully settled by the regional states for the maintenance of peace and stability.

14.   Both sides expressed their commitment to a just and comprehensive solution to the Middle East problem, which would enable the Palestinians to establish their own independent state. While supporting the legitimate aspirations of the people of Palestine for the liberation of their homeland, they called for the

vacation of all occupied Arab and Palestinian territories including Al Quds Al Sharif.

15.   Both sides expressed their concern over the continuation of the internal conflict in Afghanistan and called for a just and equitable political settlement in accordance with the aspirations of the Afghan Muslim people They also agreed to persuade the warring factions in Afghanistan to avoid further bloodshed so that the people of Afghanistan could devote themselves to the reconstruction and rehabilitation of these country. The two sides also agreed to continue consultations on the situation obtaining in Afghanistan.

16.   The two sides discussed the situation in Bosnia-Herzegovina and condemned the ethnic cleansing, genocide and massive human rights violations to which the people of Bosnia-Herzegovina have been subjected. They called for the trial and punishment of all those found guilty of serious crimes in Bosnia-Herzegovina. They further called for a complete restoration of peace in Bosnia-Herzegovina and stressed that any settlement to be just and durable must guarantee the territorial integrity, political independence and sovereignty of Bosnia-Herzegovina. They considered as unjust and illegal the U.N. arms embargo against Bosnia-Herzegovina and demanded its lifting to enable the people of Bosnia-Herzegovina to exercise their inherent right of self defence. Both sides while reiterating the continuation of their relief aid to the people of Bosnia-Herzegovina, called for the more active participation of Islamic countries in peacetime developments as well as reconstruction of Bosnia-Herzegovina.

17.   On Kashmir, the two sides exchanged views and concluded that the oppression to which the people of Kashmir were subjected remained a source of tension in the region The two sides reviewed the latest developments in the movement for self- determination by the people of Kashmir and realization of their wishes. They underlined the importance of finding a solution to the Kashmir problem in accordance with the relevant United Nations resolutions and through meaningful negotiation. President Hashemi Rafsanjani's mediation efforts were welcomed by Prime Minister Mohtarma Benazir Bhutto.

18.   The two sides deplored the aggression committed against the Republic of Azerbaijan, the occupation of Azeri territories and the explosion of hundreds of thousands of Azeri people and emphasised that steps be reversed. While expressing their satisfaction on the establishment of a ceasefire between the Republic of Azerbaijan and Armenia, they called upon the international community to be forthcoming in providing assistance for the relief and rehabilitation of Azeri refugees.

19.   Both sides noted with satisfaction the process of normalization taking place in Tajikistan. They reaffirmed that the inter-Tajik dialogue was the only means of reaching a peaceful accord. Both sides while emphasizing the necessity of expediting the holding of the fifth round of inter Tajik talks expressed their support for the UN peace efforts, as well as of concerned parties, necessary for the completion of the negotiating process. The two sides underscored the importance of national reconciliation. Tajikistan and agreed to coordinate their efforts in this regard. They also stressed the importance of efforts by the observer states concerned with the crisis in Tajikistan to accelerate the peace of talks.

20.   Both sides called for reforms of the Security Council and in context emphasized the importance of expansion in the membership of council based on the principles of "sovereign equality of states" and "equitable geographic distribution" of seats. They also emphasized that such expansion should not lead to the perpetuation of existing anomalies and creation of new centres of privilege. They recalled in this context, the relevant paragraphs of the NAM Summit Communiqué issued at Cartagena recently.

21.   The two sides reaffirmed their commitments aimed at total elimination of nuclear arsenals and other weapons of mass destruction and strengthening of the non-proliferation regime at the global and regional level. They called for intensifying of international efforts to facilitate the application of nuclear energy for peaceful purposes. They emphasized the need for enhancing the security of non-nuclear weapons states against the use or threat of use of nuclear weapons and called for the establishment of nuclear-free-zones in various parts of the world including the Middle East South Asia.

22.   Both sides discussed and exchanged views on the role of the Islamic Conference Organisation in international developments. They stressed the need for further consultation and cooperation among Islamic countries to confront the cultural and political onslaught against the Islamic World.

23.   The Prime Minister of Pakistan expressed her profound gratitude for the warm and generous hospitality extended by the President Hojjatoleslam Akbar Hashemi Rafsanjani, the Government and the people of the Islamic Republic of Iran during her visit.

 24. The Prime Minister, Mohtarma Benazir Bhutto extended an invitation to President His Excellency Hojjatoleslam Akbar Hashemi Rafsanjani to visit Pakistan in 1996. The invitation was cordially accepted. The dates for the visit would be finalized through diplomatic channels.

Source: *Foreign Affairs, November-December 1995, pp.245-250.*

APPENDIX-IV

JOINT COMMUNIQUÉ ISSUED ON THE CONCLUSION OF THE OFFICIAL VISIT OF THE PRIME MINISTER OF THE ISLAMIC REPUBLIC OF PAKISTAN TO THE ISLAMIC REPUBLIC OF IRAN (21-23 OCTOBER, 2003)

1.   His Excellency Mir Zafarullah Khan Jamali, Prime Minister of the Islamic Republic of Pakistan paid an official visit to the Islamic Republic of Iran from 21-23 October, 2003 at the invitation of His Excellency Syed Mohammad Khatami, the President of the Islamic Republic of Iran. The Prime Minister of Pakistan was accompanied by a high level delegation which included Minister for Commerce, Minister for Information and Broadcasting, Minister for Petroleum and Natural Resources and senior officials.

2.   As a reflection of the close fraternal relations between the brotherly countries of Iran and Pakistan, the Prime Minister of Pakistan was accorded a very warm and cordial welcome on arrival in Tehran.

3.   After the welcoming ceremony at the Saadabad Complex, hosted by H.E. Mr. Mohammad Reza Aref, First Vice President of the Islamic Republic of Iran, the Prime Minster of the Islamic Republic of Pakistan held official talks with President Syed Mohammad Khatami and the first Vice President of Iran, Mr. Aref in two separate sessions on 21 October. The talks held in a cordial atmosphere covered the entire range of bilateral relations as well as regional and international issues of mutual interest. Their discussions were characterized by similarity of views on important issues. Special emphasis was placed on enhancing bilateral cooperation, particularly in the economic sphere. They noted that Iran and Pakistan shared deep cultural and historical bonds, economic complementaries and

common strategic interests. They expressed deep satisfaction at the growing positive momentum in the friendly bilateral relations between Pakistan and Iran.

4.   The Prime Minister of the Islamic Republic of Pakistan paid a visit to the Mausoleum of Imam Khomeini to pay homage to late Imam. He called on the Supreme leader of Iran and had a meeting with Mr. Akbar Hashemi Rafsanjani Chairman of Expediency Council and former President of Iran. He also visited Mashed on 23rd October.

5.   The two sides expressed their determination to further strengthen the bilateral relations by enhancing closer cooperation in areas including political, security,   economic,   commercial, cultural,   information,   scientific   and technological fields.

6.   To further strengthen bilateral economic relations, they noted a number of mechanisms including a Joint Economic Commission ministerial level are already in place and a number of agreements have been signed for promotion of bilateral economic interaction. They stressed the need for full and prompt implementation of the bilateral agreements and decisions of the Joint Economic Commission.

7.   The two sides took a number of important decisions to enhance bilateral economic cooperation, including:

a)   To conclude a Preferential Trade Agreement to facilitate bilateral trade.

b)   In addition to the annual bilateral consultations, Foreign Secretary of Pakistan and Deputy Foreign Minister of Iran will meet soon to identify fresh avenues to intensify the bilateral economic cooperation.

c)   A Joint Working Committee comprising experts from energy sector will start functioning soon to finalize arrangements for construction of a gas pipeline to the Pakistan-Iranian border and its possible extension to the Pakistani territory.

d)   Iran will supply electricity to Chaghi and Dalbandin districts in Baluchistan province of Pakistan, details of which will be finalized soon.

e)   Facilitate regular exchange of economic and technical experts/delegation to intensify economic cooperation.

f)   Arrangements will be finalized soon for movement across the Pakistan-Iran   border at Panjgur and Saravan in Baluchistan province of Pakistan.

8.   Taking note of the developments at the regional and global levels, the two sides emphasized the importance of Dialogue among Civilizations and the promotion of Enlightened Moderation for constructive interaction with the West and effective cooperation within the Muslim world. They also called for the settlement of disputes by peaceful means on the basis of sovereign equality and non-interference in internal affairs of other states. They stressed the need for promotion of peace, tolerance and pluralism among civilizations and nations.

9.   Both sides called for an early resumption of unconditional dialogue between Pakistan and India for resolution of the Kashmir dispute by peaceful means in accordance with the wishes of the Kashmiri people.

10.   The two sides reiterated their support for the Bonn process and endeavours of President Karzai for national reconciliation and reconstruction of Afghanistan. They reiterated their commitment to the Kabul Declaration on Good Neighbourly Relations. They called upon the international agencies and states which attended the Tokyo meeting to honour their commitments for the reconstruction of Afghanistan. They noted the need for a broad based political dispensation in Afghanistan in keeping with the wishes of all ethnic groups. They emphasized the need for early restoration of normalcy and stability in Afghanistan to facilitate peace and security in the region.

11.   They also agreed to revive meetings of the Finance Ministers of Iran, Afghanistan and Pakistan for trilateral economic cooperation

reconstruction of Afghanistan. They also decided to enhance trilateral cooperation to combat terrorism and drug trafficking.

12.   The two sides strongly condemned the Israeli brutal suppression of the Palestinian people and denial of their fundamental rights including the tight to self-determination. They reaffirmed their commitment to early establishment of an independent Palestinian state with Al-Quds Al Sharif as its capital. They also strongly condemned the recent Israeli aggression against Syria and its aggressive designs against the Arab states which posed a grave to the peace and security in the region.

13.   Both sides expressed concern about the current situation in Iraq. They reaffirmed their commitment to the sovereignty and territorial integrity of Iraq and called for end to occupation of Iraq. They underlined that the control over the natural resources of Iraq is to be exercised by Iraq and the Governance of Iraq is the right of Iraqi people and it should be restored to them, as soon as possible. They called for a greater role by the United Nations in restoring Iraq's sovereignty and political independence.

14.   They welcomed the decision of the 10th OIC Summit for establishing a Commission for revitalization of the organization. They noted the need for making OIC an efficient, effective and efficacious, capable of realizing aspirations of the Islamic Ummah. They also re-affirmed the need for accelerating the process for regional economic integration within the ECO framework.

15.   The Prime Minister of the Islamic Republic of Pakistan expressed his appreciation for the warm welcome and the traditional hospitality extended by the President, the 1st Vice President and the people of the friendly country of Iran to him and his entourage during the visit. It was agreed between the two sides to enhance mutual interaction through regular exchange of high level visits with a view to strengthening the fraternal relations between the Islamic Republic of Pakistan and the Islamic Republic of Iran.

16.   The Prime Minister of the Islamic Republic of Pakistan extended cordial invitations to the President of the Islamic Republic of Iran and the First Vice President to pay official visits to Pakistan. The invitations were accepted with gratitude. President Khatami also

reiterated his invitation to the President of Pakistan to visit Iran in the near future. The dates of the visits will be decided later through diplomatic channels.

Source: Foreign Affairs Pakistan, Vol. XXX, Issue 10, 16-31 October 2003, pp. 154-158.

Notes:

[1] Translated by the Secreatariat of the League of Nations, for information.

[2] The ratification were deposited at Tehran, June 25th, 1938

[3] Vol.XCIV, page 57;Vol. CXXXIV, page 411; Vol. CLII, page 298; and Vol. CLX, page 354, of this Series.